UNSTOPPABLE

Published by SuccessBooks®, Lake Mary, FL.

SuccessBooks® is a registered trademark.

ISBN: 979-8-9918645-3-4
LCCN: 2025909227

This publication is designed to provide accurate and authoritative information with regard to the subject matter covered. It is sold with the understanding that the publisher is not engaged in rendering legal, accounting, or other professional advice. If legal advice or other expert assistance is required, the services of a competent professional should be sought. The opinions expressed by the authors in this book are not endorsed by SuccessBooks® and are the sole responsibility of the author rendering the opinion.

Scripture quotations marked KJV are from the King James Version of the Bible.

Scripture quotations marked NKJV are taken from the New King James Version®. Copyright © 1982 by Thomas Nelson. Used by permission. All rights reserved.

Most SuccessBooks® titles are available at special quantity discounts for bulk purchases for sales promotions, premiums, fundraising, and educational use. Special versions or book excerpts can also be created to fit specific needs.

For more information, please write:

SuccessBooks®
3415 W. Lake Mary Blvd. #950370
Lake Mary, FL 32795
or call 1.877.261.4930

Visit us online at: www.CelebrityPressPublishing.com

UNSTOPPABLE

STORIES
OF GRIT,
DETERMINATION,
AND PERSEVERANCE

SUCCESS
BOOKS
Lake Mary, FL

CONTENTS

CHAPTER 1

FAITH TESTED, AGAIN

By Lisa Nichols

One moment you're standing. The next, you're on your knees. In the afternoon you're smiling and dreaming of a bright future.

In the evening you're paralyzed by the shock of yet another setback, another violent wave threatening to pull you under.

I've been there.

I know what it's like to cry until you're empty. To scream at the sky, begging for answers.

There were moments when I believed the bruises meant I was powerless. Moments I thought the empty bank account meant I was destined for poverty. Days I believed the failures proved I wasn't worthy of success.

But here's what I know now: Resilience isn't birthed in comfort. It's forged in fire!

This is not just my story. It's proof that no matter how hard you fall, you can rise.

Resilience is not something you have to be born with. It's not a special magic reserved for the chosen few. It's a *muscle*—one you can grow and strengthen with every choice to have faith when there is no evidence that you should.

It starts with knowing your birthright.

You don't have to earn your birthright. You don't have to wait for permission to claim it. I know it's my birthright to be happy, to feel peace, to be loved, and to live in joy because I am a child of God and joy is part of my inheritance. It's *yours* too.

11

The person who gets back up is the one who believes—deep in their bones—that they have the *right* to rise. Just as you inherited your eye color or the texture of your hair, you inherited the ability to self-heal, to persevere, and to rise stronger every single time—even when you find yourself navigating the unthinkable.

God Goes to Jail with Me

Clank!

The steel door slammed shut behind me, a shocking reminder that I'd just entered a new and terrifying world. I was in *jail*, and not just any jail, but a high-security women's penitentiary because the small local precinct that I would have normally gone to happened to not have a female officer on duty that dreaded day.

I just completed working for a company that was under investigation for embezzlement. I had no idea fraud was happening right under my nose; I was just doing my job. On paper I was tangled in the mess. The court had accidentally sent my subpoena to my mother's house, where it sat, unopened, with piles of other envelopes, unopened mail she'd forgotten to give me. I had no idea that I had broken any law by not showing up to court.

So one morning as I stepped outside to go to my *first day* at my new job, two officers were waiting for me just outside my apartment door.

"Ma'am, you are being arrested for a failure-to-appear violation and have the right to remain silent…"

They cuffed me and put me in the back of a police car.

I was shocked and confused. I had just begun to rebuild my relationship with God after years of distance due to church hurt. Though I was scared, I could feel God's presence with me in the back seat of the undercover black Mustang police car that had become my prison transport. I was not alone.

I racked my brain trying to remember just *one* of my favorite gospel songs that instantly brought me peace, but my brain was completely blank, none of the songs that I would sing at sunrise worship service, Sunday service, or singles ministry Bible study would come to me. I had nothing to calm my quickly rising anxiety. So in my best tone-deaf voice, as the police car sped toward the state penitentiary, I made up my own worship song: "God is good, and good is God. Woo-hoo!"

I sang because I refused to let this take me under. If I was going to jail, I was taking God with me! I repeated that same verse over and over again until I could hear God faintly whispering into my spirit, "Everywhere you go, there I am."

For the next twenty-seven hours I sat in that prison. With over fifty women cramped into a holding room, I hummed, "God is good, and good is God. Woo-hoo!" Through fights, chaos, and constant violations, I sang even louder, "God is good, and good is God. Woo-hoo!" As the hours went by, my conviction and comfort singing out loud got even stronger. With my head bouncing from side to side and my toe tapping to my off-tune beat, the other women looked at me as if I had lost my mind. Maybe they thought I was crazy, and that was fine with me.

I kept my eyes shut tight, refusing to let the threatening conversations around me pierce my peace. "God is good, and good is God. Woo-hoo!"

In that moment, I understood something deeper than I ever had before—faith isn't just a feeling. It's not just words you speak. It's the foundation you stand on when everything else is falling apart. I knew my God was good and truth would prevail.

The next morning, they took me to court. My mother rushed in, clutching a stack of unopened envelopes to prove I hadn't seen them.

Just like that, the judge ordered my release.

After what some would consider a night in hell, I walked out the same way I walked in—singing. "God is good, and good is God. Woo-hoo!" Even in the darkest place imaginable, designed to break me, my spirit was not available to my circumstances. My spirit was unbreakable and unshakable.

THE POWER OF OWNING YOUR TRUTH

I grew up in South Central Los Angeles. I walked home from school dodging fights I never started. I learned that I should never wear jewelry and that hair kept pulled back was harder to tear out.

My house faced the police department, and some days I would sit there and watch them unload prostitutes from the paddy wagons. I knew deep in my bones that this was not the life I wanted for myself.

But as dangerous and chaotic as it was outside, in my house I had peace.

My mom was the favorite fun mom of all time, and my dad was my superhero. My favorite show was *The Brady Bunch*. There was something reassuring about watching kids grow up in a way that didn't require them to keep their head on a swivel. I was lucky enough to have parents who were loving and present. My family built a world within a world, one where love was louder than gunshots, and they were fiercely committed to protecting us from the fate of the people on the streets.

One thing I knew for sure from an early age was that I was *never* going to be with a man who was in jail. That was my greatest fear. If I ended up with a man behind bars, it meant the streets had won. I wasn't going to let that happen. I wanted my Brady Bunch!

But life has a way of testing the very things we swear we'll never do, and sometimes that test comes in the form of a handsome man!

I was working at a girls' after-school program. My computer broke one day, and in walked the computer guy—wow! Beautiful, brilliant, and single. Instantly a whirlwind romance began. I'd pick up on small conversations that left a bad taste in my mouth. I had a feeling he was close to some people who were living dirty, but he was also a math teacher and assured me that he wanted the same things I did.

I had told him from the start, "If you ever go to jail, you're on your own. I am not a jailhouse girlfriend, and I can't be tethered to prison in any way.

Thirteen months later I got pregnant, and when our son was just five months old, I got the call.

"Lisa, I'm in jail."

My worst nightmare had come true.

There I was, tethered to a man behind bars and drowning in shame because of it.

For three years I lied to my family.

"He's out of town," I'd say. "Work is keeping him away."

For three years I kept up the charade, hoping no one would discover the truth. I lived riddled in a private shame that consumed my joy.

I loved my son's father's brilliance. His ability to captivate anyone with both his written and spoken words simply left me in awe of him. He would go on to author twenty-six books from prison—*four before I even published my first*. He would become a man of deep wisdom, transformation, and influence—I carried the burden of his choices as if they were mine. I wore the cloak of guilt for my son's fatherless experience; for years I let shame keep me silent.

I let the fear of what people would think dictate how much of my truth I was willing to share.

I ended the relationship, but I carried the weight of my own self-judgment. I was convinced that if people knew, they would doubt my ability to lead.

I made myself smaller, shared half my passion, spoke timidly with only a fraction of my power.

But here's the thing about purpose: When you are *called*, you *cannot hide.*

God will keep placing signs in front of you until you listen.

For me those signs came in the form of opportunities to write books—first, *Chicken Soup for the African American Soul*, then *Chicken Soup for the African American Woman's Soul*, and then *The Secret*.

There was one opportunity after another, all declaring, "You don't get to hide in the shadows, Lisa Nichols!"

We are all here on a divine assignment, and you cannot fulfill your calling if you're drowning in shame.

So I did the work. I lit candles. I cried for hours. I *wrote* the story of the truth I'd buried for too long. I had to own every part of my journey because my purpose required courage.

Shame is a myth.

It's a lie we tell ourselves when we believe our past disqualifies us from greatness. But your past is not your prison; it's your *classroom*!

Shame only has power if you let it keep you silent. The moment you *own* your story is the moment you step into your true power. Power that will be tested again and again, as it was for me when I met the man I thought I would marry…and woke up to his hands around my neck.

Trust Yourself, Value Yourself, and Never Ignore the Signs

He was everything a woman was supposed to want—charming, thoughtful, romantic. We were planning our wedding, and he treated me like a queen.

In the back of my mind there were whispers. Tiny moments that made my stomach tighten. Little things that didn't sit quite right. I even had dreams that he tried to kill me, but in the light of day they seemed ridiculous. I was more committed to making it work than to listening to my gut, and his behavior fed my denial.

He was love-bombing me with flowers, gifts for Jelani, and beautiful words, and I had no reason to fear him. I told myself maybe I was imagining things.

One night after a beautiful date during which he bathed me and treated me like a queen, we fell into bed, made love, and drifted to sleep in each other's arms.

At 3:20 a.m., I woke to his hands around my throat.

No fight. No argument. No reason.

Just his hands cutting off my air and tightening around my neck with every move I made.

I tried to process what was happening, but darkness closed in, and I passed out.

When I woke up, I thought I was dead at first, and then reality set in, followed by absolute panic.

Where was my son? My three-year-old baby had been sleeping in the next room. I ran, screaming for him, my heart pounding, and when I reached him, he lay there unmoving.

I shattered.

"God, if my son is dead, you might as well have let him kill me too."

And then his tiny eyes fluttered open. "Mommy?"

I sobbed with relief. But as tears ran down my face, I knew—I had to get out. No matter what. Even if he apologized, cried, and swore it would never happen again.

But if he didn't apologize? If he acted as if nothing happened?

Then I was in *real* trouble.

I walked downstairs, bracing myself and expecting to see guilt on his face. Instead, he turned around, calm as ever, and said, "Good morning, baby. I made you breakfast."

For a split second, I wondered if I had imagined it, but then I went to the bathroom, pulled my robe down, and saw deep burgundy bruises around my throat.

I knew right then and there that I was in the fight of my life.

For three months I played along, pretending everything was fine, slowly plotting my escape, an escape that became urgent the day he lifted me by my neck and hurled me across the room. I convinced him to visit his family three thousand miles away for five weeks as one long family-connection vacation before the wedding.

The moment he left, I moved out, changed jobs, and excommunicated all of his friends.

That's when I learned the truth—he was severely bipolar and had stopped taking his medication when he moved to California, believing that love could cure his illness. I was finally physically safe, but my body was not all that had been assaulted. My soul and my trust in myself had taken a beating too, and eventually, a doctor prescribed depression medication.

Me! Depressed! I made my living motivating people, so I could not let this situation consume me. I did what I should have done from the start.

I valued *myself*.

I wrote my own personal prescription for feeling better, doing mirror work, writing personal affirmations, and leaning on God. It was not overnight; it took a while and much intentional work on myself, but eventually, I forgave myself for ignoring the signs, and I began to remind myself that my heart and soul were worthy of care.

Thirteen years later I was speaking on stage in front of 350 people, and out of the blue I saw him standing in the back of the room.

Panic hit me; I was instantly thrown back into all my greatest fear storms. I instantly decided to give every person a refund and run for shelter. "God, I can't do this." And God whispered back, "Yes, you can; wherever you go, there I am."

I decided to trust God more than I trusted myself. OK, here we go—"God is good, and good is God. Woo-hoo!" I even surprised myself with the strength and conviction of my message as my abuser stood gazing at me during the final portion of my speech. After my talk a woman approached me: "Please," she said, "give my husband back to me."

It was his wife. She told me he was riddled with guilt and had never forgiven himself for what he had done. I walked up to him, and there were tears streaming down his face. Wait! Monsters don't cry, and in every version of my story of him, he's the monster. In that moment, I didn't see a villain but a hurting man.

And in that Atlanta convention center, with three hundred people witnessing, I released him, and in doing so released myself.

When I look back, I don't blame myself for wanting to believe in love. I don't blame myself for seeing the best in someone.

But I will never again ignore my intuition.

Because intuition is a gift.

How many times do we feel tiny nudges in our guts that

something is off, but we wait for a sign. Your spirit speaking *is* the sign! You don't need the neon billboard or the lightning strike. Your intuition is the voice of the Holy Spirit speaking directly to you!

When you value yourself enough to believe that God makes time to speak to you, you don't wait for the *bigger* sign—you trust the whisper.

Because you are worthy of peace. You are worthy of love. And most of all—you are worthy of a life you never have to escape.

Life will try to convince you that you belong on the ground. It will hit you with heartbreak or a setback so deep it turns your world upside down. It will tell you that you are too broken, too tired, too old, or too late to rise again, and for a moment, you might believe it, but remember this: The person who rises again does so because they *believe* they have the *right* to rise.

That doesn't mean it will be easy. Somewhere along the way, we've confused difficulty with denial. We think because the road is steep, we're not meant to climb it. Because the door is heavy, we're not supposed to push through it. But faith doesn't mean you won't get knocked down, only that you're built to get back up.

We build muscle only when we add resistance. You wouldn't know the power of your own voice if you were never silenced, or the depth of your courage if fear never stood in your path.

I am where I am today because I've risen more times than I've fallen. If I've made it farther, it's because every time I hit the ground, I decided—right then and there—that the ground was no place for me to stay.

You are not meant to live life on your knees. You are not meant to hide from the storms but to charge through them with faith as your shelter. You were not meant to settle for scraps but to receive in abundance.

So stand up.

Stand tall.

Stand again and again as many times as it takes until you finally remember and claim your birthright—as a descendant of the divine, as a bottomless well of strength, and as an unstoppable force of light, love, and resilience.

About Lisa

Lisa Nichols is one of the world's most-requested speakers, as well as media personality and corporate CEO, whose global platform reaches over 170 countries and serves over 80 million people. Lisa's social media reach is over 2.4 million followers.

As Founder and Chief Executive Officer of Motivating the Masses, Inc., Lisa has helped develop workshops and programs that have transformed thousands of businesses, and the lives of entrepreneurs. As a result of her training, her students become unforgettable speakers, best-selling authors, and 6 and 7-figure entrepreneurs.

Lisa's extraordinary story of transforming her own life from public assistance to leading a multi-million-dollar enterprise is the inspiration behind her bold mission to teach others that it is possible to do the same. Today, fans worldwide revere Lisa for her mastery of teaching people how to accomplish unfathomable goals and tap into their limitless potential.

CHAPTER 2

YOU ARE IN CHARGE OF YOU!

By Patricia Scipio, DPS

The key wouldn't turn.

I jiggled it, took it out, tried it again. I turned it left, then right, my hand starting to shake as I glanced over my shoulder to see if anyone was watching. The key worked just fine yesterday. Standing there with a plastic grocery bag in one hand and a key that refused to turn in the other, I knew something was wrong—the kind of wrong that makes your heart stop and your stomach drop.

This was *my* home. My sanctuary. The place I'd been so proud to call my own. The day I turned eighteen, I had moved out of the cramped apartment in the Bronx where I shared very little space with five siblings, all fighting for privacy, fighting for the TV, fighting for space on the only couch we owned.

I tried again. Maybe it was just jammed. I knelt to peer at the lock, my pulse gaining speed as the truth began to set in.

They'd changed the lock.

I was two days late on rent. Two days. I was a good tenant and thought for sure they would have called or left a note if my tardiness was going to be a problem. But no. Clearly the homeowner didn't care about grace periods or compassion. The rent was late, and I was out with no warning, no plan B, and no sympathy.

Everything I owned—my favorite clothes, my important documents, the few things I treasured most—was locked behind that door. My pride and sense of independence evaporated instantly.

I stood there, stunned, as the realization set in. The only option was the one I had vowed never to take: going back to my parents' apartment in the projects.

I blinked back tears as I made my way back to the life I had spent years trying to get out of. At that moment, as I walked home, the streets of that Bronx neighborhood seemed to taunt me and reflect to me my own failure. Yet something else was happening too. A fire was lit within, and I made myself a promise: never again.

Never again would I be at the mercy of someone else's decisions. Never again would I let myself be powerless. From that day forward I swore I would take care of myself, no matter what it took.

No one would ever lock me out of my own life again.

You're Hired!

They say that failure is nothing more than success in progress.

One thing I learned over the years is that it doesn't matter how trained you are, how prepared you think you are, or how hard you work—sometimes failure is inevitable. The key is to leverage it into success; the challenge is that no one teaches you *how*.

Most of us can rattle off some algebra terms, a few elements on the periodic table, and other random facts we learned in school, but the curriculum fell short when it came to teaching the principles of success, and that's because it cannot be learned from a book.

Success is forged through experience and in most cases through failures.

When I was locked out of my home, I realized that a high school diploma and a minimum-wage job wasn't going to cut it. I needed a college degree. I could have decided that I had failed to live on my own, but instead, I decided that I had succeeded in learning what *didn't* work!

While I didn't realize it at the time, I was learning to become the CEO of my own life!

Becoming the CEO of your own life is about stepping into a role of leadership over every aspect of your existence. Think of your life as a company—you have your mission, your values, your team, your policies and procedures, and your bottom line. As the CEO, you hold the power to decide who gets a seat at the table—who aligns with your vision and lifts you higher—and who no longer belongs in your boardroom. You define the mission statement, chart the one-year, five-year, and ten-year plans, and take charge of your most valuable asset: your mind. As the CEO of your life, you don't just manage the day-to-day—you shape your destiny.

I've been lucky to have a successful forty-five-year career as a leader in some of the best-in-class organizations as their internal audit, risk management, accounting, and compliance expert. I retired and launched my consulting and coaching business, sharing all the growth principles I've learned over the years to help others reach their full potential.

Here's what I know for sure: Principles of expansion and abundance are the same no matter where they are applied. Everything that grows a business grows *you* too!

You've got to decide on your personal policies and procedures. You've got to have a strong financial mindset. You've got to "hire" the team of people you want around you and "fire" the ones you don't.

A business will zero in on its unique value proposition, and so should you.

Essentially, what grows a business grows the self.

I'd like to offer you the role of CEO in your life. Congratulations. You're hired!

CEOs Use Failure as a Strategy for Growth

In 2001 I was enjoying a successful time in my career. I was a vice president at a large company with a team of more than one hundred people reporting to me. My gleaming office was set against the stunning backdrop of the Manhattan skyline, on the twenty-ninth floor of the World Trade Center.

Just that morning, I had made my way into the building, admiring the view of the Twin Towers as I approached them, noticing how beautifully the sun was shining on their windows and feeling so grateful to be walking through those doors.

Of course, we had no idea that just a couple of hours later, thousands would be dead and life would be forever changed.

The images are permanently etched on my mind. I gathered my team and led them down the stairs in a single-file line as the firemen, brows pouring with sweat and bodies heavy with gear, were walking up the stairs to their death.

The days and months after were dark and uncertain. I accounted for every member of my team and set up temporary office space in hotel rooms. Eventually my whole team was laid off and my function was outsourced.

I had been kicked off the mountain again, and it wouldn't be the last time. It was up to me to lead my team through this devastating collection of losses and point their vision toward a future no one could see through the haze of smoke and debris.

Yet just as the great city of New York rebuilt itself stronger in the aftermath of unexpected loss, so can we. Change is, after all, an inevitable part of life. If we aren't changing, we aren't growing, and if we aren't growing, we're dying!

The universe, it seemed, wasn't ever going to let me get complacent. Every time I would get comfortable in a job, change would step in and move me. We see these things as bad luck, but really they are divine redirection.

The job that didn't work out, the relationship that ended unexpectedly, or the promotion that went to someone else are all gifts that feel like curses, all perceived failures that are actually moving us closer to our next success.

You see, failure is just energy in motion—a messenger delivering the wisdom we need to grow. It's not a reflection of who we are but a gentle (or sometimes not-so-gentle) nudge toward something greater. When we release the need to tie our identity to what didn't work, failure becomes an ally, not an enemy.

This is a lesson that would repeat for me over and over, even before graduating from college with a degree in accounting. I had landed an excellent job with a major public accounting firm. This job had a well-defined, structured career path, but I was not promoted with my class in my first year at the company. I was devastated. My only goal for the second year at the firm was to pass all four parts of the CPA exam. I collaborated with other professionals, joined study groups, and stayed focused. Not only did I ace the exam within my two-year period, but I immediately found another position in a better corporate environment.

Failure isn't rejection—it's redirection. It's the universe reminding us to pivot, to rise, and to trust that every closed door is a breadcrumb leading us closer to our highest potential. Every chapter that ends is an invitation to start writing a new one. Think of every piece of "bad luck" as the universe stepping in as mama bird and pushing you out of the nest—not so you can fall but so you can *fly*.

CEOs Create Opportunities Where None Exist

Opportunities don't always come gift wrapped and handed to us. Sometimes we have to create them. If opportunities aren't naturally built into your current world, don't wait for someone to give you permission to lead. Give yourself permission. Hire *yourself*!

That's what being the CEO of your life is all about—recognizing that your growth, success, and leadership are in *your* hands, even when the road isn't paved for you.

I've always been a lifelong learner. I've soaked up wisdom from mentors such as Oprah, Tony Robbins, and, most recently, Lisa Nichols. But here's the truth: Reading and learning alone didn't transform my life. The real change came when I decided to intentionally place myself in situations where I could grow, lead, and shine.

One of the biggest lessons I've learned is that leadership doesn't have to come from a title or a job description. In the corporate world you don't always get handed leadership roles. But when I started volunteering in affinity groups and professional associations, I discovered a whole new world of opportunity. Suddenly I wasn't just attending meetings—I was running them. I wasn't just part of the crowd—I was at the front of the room.

These roles weren't about paychecks or promotions, and I did all of them for free. For me they were about growth. They gave me skills I never would have gained had I waited for someone in HR to push me up a ladder. Instead, I went out of my way to be part of groups that taught me how to lead a team, communicate effectively, and build meaningful connections. What's more, these groups became my secret weapon. They opened doors to new opportunities because I stayed connected with people and organizations that saw my potential.

When I look back, the moments that transformed my life weren't the ones handed to me—they were the ones I created. I intentionally placed myself in spaces where I could lead, learn, and connect. By doing this, I didn't just grow my skills; I expanded my vision of what was possible.

You have the same power. The only thing standing between you and the opportunities you dream of is your willingness to step up and make them happen. You don't need a fancy title or an invitation to shine—you just need the courage to say, "I'm ready."

What room can you walk into, what role can you take on, and what action can you say yes to? When you choose to lead, you're not just creating more work for yourself—you're creating a life that reflects, and ultimately unlocks, your highest potential.

CEOs Get Up, Again and Again

I worked long, hard days and weekends, deferred vacations, and missed holidays with family to rise to the position of corporate controller. Me, a poor girl from the Bronx, had worked her way up to one of the highest positions in a huge company.

One day I got to work and was told I wasn't needed anymore. I was not given a reason, and to this day I don't know what happened. All I knew was that one minute I was at the top of my career, and the next minute I was kicked off the ladder and landing with a thud on the floor.

I had been in the corporate world long enough to know that decisions like this were made all the time, but that didn't soften the blow, and that gut punch brought with it a period of intense depression. Mentally, it felt like being back at that door, jiggling the key over and over, panic setting in. Another door closed and locked.

But then I remembered, the closed doors are actually promotions.

I may have been fired from that position, but I was repeatedly promoted to CEO of my life!

You can take my title, but you can never take *me*. My education, my character, my grit—those are untouchable. You can kick me out of a corporate role, but I'm still my own boss.

Through every moment of despair or every unexpected change, I can always take full responsibility for my choices and my future. I can always seek mentors and coaches who challenge me, push me, and teach me. I can always immerse myself in stories of high achievers who faced unimaginable obstacles and draw strength from their resilience.

I can always set new personal goals and write new stories, embracing every plot twist as a gift or invitation.

That's what taking control of your own life is all about. It's not about avoiding failure—it's about rising after every fall. It's about seeing closed doors not as endings but as promotions to something greater.

A kid will build a tower of blocks, watch it crumble, and rebuild it over and over, each time stacking those blocks higher and higher even though that increases the likelihood of it all crashing down.

Now that's determination we can all learn from.

So yes, I lost that corporate title, but I gained something far more valuable: the clarity to see that my ultimate title—CEO of my life—was never up for grabs. And neither is yours.

No matter what life throws at you, remember this: The only ladder that matters is the one you build *yourself.* And when you climb it, don't be surprised to find that the view is even better than you imagined.

About Patricia

Patricia Scipio, DPS, is a powerhouse in corporate leadership, renowned for her ability to turn complex challenges into opportunities for growth and success. With a career spanning professional services, multinational corporations, nonprofits, and public agencies, Dr. Scipio is celebrated for her unparalleled expertise in risk management, compliance, and internal audit.

As a strategic leader, Scipio has shaped the risk strategies of global organizations, driving accountability, operational excellence, and innovation across industries such as health care, higher education, government contracting, and legal services. Her impact is measured not just in results but in the lasting frameworks she builds—designed to empower teams, enhance governance, and champion best practices.

Scipio's passion for learning is the foundation of her success. She earned her bachelor of business administration from Bernard M. Baruch College, an executive MBA from Columbia University, and a doctor of professional studies from Pace University. Her groundbreaking research on the Sarbanes-Oxley Act, published in the Library of Congress, highlights her thought leadership in financial governance. She also holds a suite of prestigious certifications, including CPA, CIA, CFE, and credentials in health care compliance and ethics.

A committed member of numerous professional organizations, Scipio has served on boards and committees, including as audit committee chair for nonprofit organizations. These roles reflect her deep dedication to advancing ethical leadership and fostering meaningful change.

Scipio expanded her transformational impact by completing an intensive Certified Transformational Trainer Program led by world-class coaches Lisa Nichols and Sean Smith. Inspired by the motto "Only transformed people can help transform others," she stepped into a new chapter as an independent consultant and coach. Today, she empowers business owners and individuals to achieve their boldest professional and personal goals, helping them unlock their potential and embrace purposeful growth.

Whether you're seeking to elevate your organization or embark on a personal journey of transformation, Scipio is here to guide you with proven strategies, unparalleled expertise, insight, and inspiration.

For more information, email Info@DrPScipio.com or visit www. DrPScipio.com.

CHAPTER 3

PROGRESS, NOT PERFECTION

By Dr. Amber O'Neill Smith

"He's…gone."

I stared at my mother but was unable to speak, her words landing like a foreign language I would never be able to make sense of.

I was eleven years old, and my father, our family's hero, was gone.

My parents had always been a source of love and positivity for me, and I was Daddy's little girl. My father had been in the army and then had gone on to be a welder. When he lost his job, he went back to school to study agriculture, and I, his constant shadow, went with him, following him down a path to the dreams he believed were within reach—not just for him but for me too.

I was so proud to go on field trips to see cows with him, and while other kids were playing outside, I was content to sit beside my father as he did his homework, fascinated as he explained what he was learning and what it could mean for us.

"If you keep going to school, Amber, you can be anything," he would say, his eyes shining. "You could even be Dr. Amber!"

And I believed him, every word.

After Dad died, my family felt forever fractured. We did our best, but my father's absence hung in the air with a heaviness that took a major toll on my mom. She had relied on my father's help to care for me and my younger sister who had special needs, and the stress of doing it all alone was a crushing weight.

As I got older, I turned my grief into a conviction that made me on a good day strong-willed, and on a bad one, stubborn as a mule! The belief my dad had instilled turned into a headstrong determination to forge my own path.

During my childhood we provided foster care to several kids, and one of them was a teenager who had become emancipated from her parents. That sounded pretty good to me, so at four-teen years old, I moved out of my mother's house, rented a studio apartment in a bad part of town, and became determined to live on my own.

It wasn't long before I found out why fourteen-year-olds shouldn't live without protection, but I refused to go home. At sixteen I petitioned the court (with my mother's help) and was granted total emancipation.

The gift my father gave me was a vision. In this vision I was strong, fearless, and highly educated.

As a first-generation college graduate, the pathway to academic success wasn't easy or direct. It would surprise a lot of people who know me professionally as Dr. Amber O'Neill Smith that gradu-ating high school initially felt insurmountable. It can be hard to imagine a future for which you have no model to follow, but my dad believed in me. His unwavering optimism and faith in me gave me the strength to keep going.

I made up my mind as an eleven-year-old girl that I would honor his memory by honoring the dream he planted. I would become Dr. Amber no matter what it took.

I just had no idea it would take so much.

BACK TO SCHOOL

Have you ever looked in a mirror and not recognize the face staring back at you?

That's what happened with me the moment I knew my mar-riage was over. I looked in the mirror and could no longer find the fiery, determined girl I had been. The spark in her eyes was gone, and I was determined to bring her back. For years I had told myself that things would get better, but now, as a mother, I knew the truth: This wasn't the life I envisioned for my child—or for me.

I knew that leaving meant starting completely over, and my dreams felt like distant stars—visible but unreachable. I had never forgotten the seed my father planted when he told me I'd one day be Dr. Amber. It had taken root deep in my soul, surviving years of doubt and hardship, but now, as a single mom living below poverty level, it seemed laughable. My dream was crazy, or so people kept telling me.

Determined to keep moving forward, I started offering childcare in my home to make ends meet. That's when I met Michele, the mother of one of the children I cared for. We became fast friends, bonded by the shared chaos of motherhood. One evening I confessed my dream to her: I wanted to go back to school, to reclaim the life I'd once imagined for myself.

"Let's do it!" she said.

Her belief was contagious, and a few weeks later we did it. We enrolled together, diving headfirst into classes, study sessions, and the endless juggling act of single motherhood. We registered for the same classes and bought one copy of each textbook to share. For a while it felt possible, as though I might just beat the odds, but reality has a way of creeping in to test our resolve. The demands of keeping a roof over our heads and food on the table while juggling a rigorous course load began to take their toll.

When the phone rang on my birthday, I assumed it was someone calling to wish me a happy birthday. Instead, the voice on the other end was clinical and emotionless.

It was the administrator of the school. She told me that I wasn't meeting expectations. I was out of the program.

I hung up the phone, stunned and devastated, feeling for a brief moment that it was all over and I had let my father down. After a few weeks, however, I could feel the spark within me light up again.

I looked around at my life—single mom, no money, no help

except for the faith my best friend had in me—and realized that yes, my dream was crazy. But maybe crazy was exactly what I needed to be.

I went online and applied to three psychology programs. I was accepted and chose to focus on international psychology.

Today, I *am* Dr. Amber!

I have been a doula for almost thirty-three years now. I am also a psychologist who specializes in perinatal resilience (pregnancy, birth, postpartum). My doctoral degree is in the emerging psychological field of international psychology with a focus on trauma and resilience.

I didn't know it at the time, but as I walked the path from a grieving child to an emancipated teen to a single mother to a PhD graduate, I was forming my own principles of unstoppable resilience. And now I'd like to share them with you.

HOLD YOUR VISION TIGHT

Ask any child what they want to be when they grow up, and you'll likely be taken on a wild ride. It never occurs to them that they can't be anything they want to be.

Doctor.

Astronaut.

Circus performer.

All of it seems valid and inevitable to their uncorrupted minds. Then, sadly, reality sneaks in. Expectations push our childhood visions to the back corners of our minds, and eventually, responsibilities, heartache, and exhaustion snuff them out completely—except for one memory that stays alive to remind you of who you were before the world got hold of you. That's the memory we need to find and grab on to!

When I work with people who are feeling disconnected and empty, I often suggest that they revisit the vision they had for themselves as a child. What did you like to play? Where did you go in your daydreams? Who did you see yourself becoming?

What did you want before you believed in limitations? Before you were trained to be "realistic?"

In my childhood I wanted to learn and help people. I wanted to be Dr. Amber, and my ability to hold tightly to that vision saw me through the most trying times. Every challenge was a necessary test on the way to my vision becoming a reality. Your vision is your anchor, and if you can train yourself to believe that it will inevitably come true, nothing can stop you.

And thank goodness for that because most of the time our visions are not just for ourselves.

A couple of years ago I was working on my PhD dissertation and had planned to interview sixteen women living in the Philippines who had been pregnant and given birth during COVID. The area had sustained record rainfall, and the roads were largely washed away by rushing water, making them virtually impassible by car. On the day I was scheduled to interview these sixteen moms, I expected to have to cancel. Instead, every single one of them showed up to talk to me. Some arrived on boats. Others came by motorcycle. A few even walked miles with their babies. They were determined to come and share their stories, and as I listened, I was so grateful for their generosity, inspired by their strength, but beyond that, I was proud—proud that I hadn't given up.

I had a mission to uplift mothers. If we can uplift, empower, and encourage mothers during pregnancy and the first one thousand days, we can change the infant's trajectory toward thriving despite early-life adversity.

My vision of becoming Dr. Amber was now playing a part in empowering *their* vision for a better life!

BORROW RESILIENCE

There are moments in life when the weight of our reality feels unbearable, and the belief we once had in ourselves begins to fade. In those moments, we can lean on the strength and unwavering faith of those who see something in us that we cannot see in ourselves.

For me, it was my father first, and then my best friend, who encouraged me to enroll in school even when I had no evidence that I could succeed.

Had she not lent me her faith, I may never have become the person I am today.

Together we studied, we shared textbooks, we kept each other going on the most challenging days, and years later, as I traveled and studied the resilience of other cultures, I would realize how integral her support had been in my journey. You see, in many cultures resilience is not seen as an individual trait but as a shared resource, woven into the fabric of the community. I've learned that in these places, the well-being of the individual is insepa-rable from the well-being of the group. Challenges are not faced alone; they are carried collectively. When one person stumbles, the others step in, not as an act of charity but as an act of mutual survival and shared humanity. This perspective shifts the weight of resilience from solitary shoulders to a communal embrace, proving that strength grows exponentially when shared.

Each of us can learn to borrow resilience. Whether it's a friend you can count on, a past achievement that acts as evidence of your success, or a memory of someone else's belief in you, draw on those things when your own well of courage runs dry.

RAISE YOUR STANDARDS

As I think back to the moment I left my marriage, I realize that it wasn't courage pushing me along but self-respect.

I had learned by contrast that I wanted *more* for myself and my child.

One of the most powerful elements of resilience is the decision to raise our standards. When we refuse to settle, even when the road is hard, we affirm our self-worth. We declare that we deserve a life of purpose, growth, and fulfillment.

To truly embrace this, ask yourself what you would want for someone you love. Would you want them to stay in a place that dims their light or accept less than they deserve? Would you cheer them on if they settled for "good enough" instead of the extraordinary life they're capable of?

When I was a young mother, I struggled through working full time, raising children, and going to school. I took a risk and applied for scholarships and grants I wasn't sure I would ever be considered for. To my amazement I was chosen as a Ford Scholar and was able to focus on my education while running my in-home day care and raising my beautiful children.

Raising our standards is an act of self-respect that requires us to step out of our comfort zones and take a chance on ourselves. When you lead with that kind of belief in yourself, you inspire those around you to rise too. True resilience is fueled by the quiet but relentless belief that you are worth every effort, every ounce of courage it takes to hold out for the life you truly deserve.

THE EMBER WITHIN US

There is a community I worked with in the Philippines that held preschool in a garbage dump. In South Africa, I had the honor of working with people who lived in haphazardly constructed homes in the slums across the street from pristine and luxurious shopping malls, thousands of people all sharing one water source. And yet they came together, they held a vision of joy, they focused on what they had rather than what they lacked, and they *persevered*.

If you've ever blown out a candle, you might notice that once in a while a tiny ember refuses to be blackened. Blow on it again, and instead of going out, it burns a little brighter, stubbornly holding on to its glow, refusing to relinquish its purpose.

That ember exists in all of us.

My father planted that ember within me, and every challenge I faced was fuel that made it burn brighter.

The path to becoming Dr. Amber was neither straight nor

smooth. It was forged through grief, determination, and the unwavering faith of those who walked beside me. It taught me that resilience is both a personal and collective strength—a force that connects us, carries us, and makes us unstoppable.

So hold on to your vision, lean on others when you need to, and never stop rising. The journey may be daunting, but the legacy you create will be worth every step. Most importantly, remember to light the ember in others any chance you get. Your words may be the spark that reawakens someone else's resolve.

And that's how together, one determined heart at a time, we can change the world.

About Amber

Dr. Amber O'Neill Smith is an esteemed scholar and advocate in the emerging field of perinatal mental health, holding a doctorate in international psychology from the Chicago School of Professional Psychology, where she specialized in trauma and resilience. With over thirty years of experience supporting mothers around the globe through pregnancy, birth, and the postpartum period, Amber's work has significantly influenced academic research in addition to both national and international public policy.

Her commitment to advocating for maternal and infant well-being is reflected in her recent publications, her dissertation titled "Perinatal Well-Being: Sociological Factors Contributing to Resilience Amidst the Covid-19 Pandemic," and "Global Mental Health Inequities: Social Determinants of Mental Health, Cultural Expectations and Gender" published by Columbia University. A member of several multicultural organizations, including the Latina Leadership Community College Council and the International Center for Traditional Childbearing (ICTC), she is a certified full-circle doula dedicated to promoting resiliency in diverse communities.

Amber's extensive educational background includes a bachelor of arts in psychology with minors in physics and Spanish from Marylhurst University, postbaccalaureate studies in the master of social work program at Portland State University, a play-therapy certificate, and a master of science in child and adolescent psychology from Capella University.

Her advocacy extends across community, state, federal, and international levels, where she has served as a Court Appointed Special Advocate (CASA) for infants and offers consultations to foster parents and group homes for developmentally delayed children. Additionally, she volunteers at her local children's hospital and provides support to families with premature infants in the neonatal intensive care unit (NICU). She is often on call with Children's Disaster Services as a child life specialist.

Amber has actively engaged in policy advocacy with organizations such as the ZERO TO THREE public policy network and has campaigned for crucial funding for programs such as Head Start and WIC nutrition programs.

Recently, she represented Oregon with Mom Congress in Washington, DC, to support legislation enhancing maternal and infant mental health and was an Oregon state representative at the national Prenatal to Three public policy conference.

An international resilience expert, Amber has shared her insights as a guest speaker across multiple nations, including Guyana, Jamaica, Mexico, South Africa, Cuba, the Philippines, and Costa Rica. Her passion and dedication to improving perinatal mental health and wellness continue to inspire change and support for mothers and infants worldwide.

Learn more at info@doctor-amber.com.

CHAPTER 4

CRAZY UNTIL IT'S NOT

The Thin Line Between Impossibility and Success

By Nick Nanton

The melody of the park carousel was the perfect background music for the laughter of the children that day. A man sat on a wooden bench, smiling as he watched his little girl ride the colorful horses.

As the carousel turned, an idea began to form in his mind—a huge and wild idea. He wondered what it might be like to create a place that captured that kind of childlike magic and joy, a place where families from all around the world could gather and for a short time be wrapped in magic and hope.

When he shared his dream, people laughed. His brother refused to help him. His friends called him crazy and warned that he'd lose everything if he chased this impossible idea. But the memory of that day in the park stayed with him, and Walt Disney used that memory to fuel his idea, willing it to grow and grow until the impossible became real.

I am far from Walt Disney; he was one of the greatest creative geniuses to ever live. But I know what it feels like to have an idea that others can't see. Over the past couple of decades, I've had the privilege of enjoying many once-in-a-lifetime experiences, and each of those began from the seed of a crazy idea. You see, often the line between crazy and visionary is just one step forward.

And my life is certainly a testament that taking that step can lead to some wild adventures!

KEEP KNOCKING

When a child tells people they're going to be a singer, an actor, or the CEO of their own business, they're usually met with amused smiles and words of encouragement.

When that same child repeats that dream out loud as an adult, they get blank stares and unsolicited advice to "get real." When do we stop believing that anything is possible?

I read a quote somewhere that struck me right in the heart. It said, "Every creative I know was told by numerous people that they should be realistic. Every single one. The songs we love, the movies we watch, and the books we read were all created by people who didn't listen."

I realized then that what most creatives have in common isn't creativity—it's *courage*—the courage to quiet the noise, abandon the need for external validation, and keep knocking on doors no matter how many are slammed shut.

They have the courage to be the "crazy outcast" in a sea of people living "normal" lives.

The people who care about us the most are often the loudest naysayers. They feel their job is to protect us from failure. What they don't realize is that they are also protecting us from success.

The legendary Jack Canfield once told me that if you have a dream, assume it was given to you by God. Would you let anything stop you if you knew your dream was a mission fully funded and backed by God?

I wouldn't!

I may need to learn a new skill or persist in the face of adversity, but I believe that if an idea was whispered to me, it's because I'm the person meant to bring it to life. It's a kind of divine assignment.

Who am I to refuse that?

Do you have a dream or idea that feels too big to be possible? A book you want to write? A city you want to move to? A company you want to start?

If so, your mission, should you choose to accept it, is to follow the path of the crazy, outcast creatives who balk at the critics, ignore the skeptics, and charge forward into the lives they were meant to live!

EMBRACE GOOD STRUGGLE

A few years ago one of these dreams was whispered to me. I had seen several Broadway shows and had seen Mike Tyson's one-man show on Netflix. It was a fascinating look at his life, and it was all performed by just him and some mixed media to back him. It reminded me of a great speech but produced to the highest level. I had spent a lot of my career working with some of the greatest speakers in the world. The idea of bringing a real story to life on stage in the heart of the Big Apple captivated me. But if I had listened to logic—or the doubters—there's no way I should've even been allowed near that dream. I had no experience, a couple of distant connections, and no blueprint. And yet against all odds we launched two successful shows, with a third on the horizon. By the time you read this, I will have produced Broadway shows featuring Rudy Ruettiger, Lisa Nichols, and Chris Voss!

These weren't traditional Broadway productions by any stretch. People told me, "You don't know what you're doing." They said, "That's not how it works." I encountered barrier after barrier.

The so-called gatekeepers insisted our one-person shows weren't real Broadway productions. There was no singing, no cast, no multi-week run. In their minds Broadway meant musicals or plays with dialogue, elaborate sets, and a full ensemble. But none of those things define Broadway; they're just common features. My shows didn't fit their mold, but they were performed in Broadway theaters, they were worked by Broadway unions, the tickets were sold where Broadway tickets were sold, and they met all the conditions of a true Broadway show. That made them Broadway shows!

Here's the thing about pursuing a dream: When it's just a vision, no one can see what you see. And that's OK. I decided this dream wasn't something I conjured up on a whim—it was a vision God gave me. I wasn't going to let roadblocks stop me.

Part of being unstoppable is facing the resistance that comes with trying to do something new. Roadblocks aren't signs to quit—they're invitations to grow. If I were perfectly emotionally mature (which I'm not), I might even welcome each one with a resounding "Yes, another challenge to conquer!"

It's not easy to feel that way in the moment. However, there's an unmatched satisfaction in solving your way through a seemingly insurmountable problem.

Ray Dalio, in his book *Principles*, talks about this idea. He says people often believe life is about success and achievement. But here's the truth: If you set out to achieve your biggest goal and the journey was too easy, it wouldn't feel fulfilling. The purpose of life isn't just about reaching the destination. It's about embracing the *good struggle*—the kind of challenge that stretches your limits, allows you to gather evidence of what you're capable of, and tests your commitment to your dreams.

Good struggle (a term coined by Dalio that I absolutely love) is the place where dreams become reality and where we become the people worthy of achieving them. Each roadblock is a step closer to mastery. Every moment of doubt is an opportunity to recommit to the vision only you can see.

So, the next time you find yourself staring down a seemingly impossible barrier, don't let fear convince you that the struggle isn't worth it. Solve your way through it. Embrace the struggle, because on the other side of it is growth, fulfillment, and the dream that was placed on your heart for a reason.

NO DOESN'T ALWAYS MEAN NO

It was 1939, and a group of young boys living at the Alabama School for the Negro Deaf and Blind were about to change the music industry forever. A group of friends formed a singing group and began sneaking away from the school to sing at churches and small military training camps. They had no connections and no reason to think they could gain any kind of success outside of their small town. But by the 1950s The Blind Boys of Alabama was the leading gospel group in the country.

The problem was that the demand for gospel music was declining as rhythm and blues swept the nation. For years they struggled and faced the challenges of poverty, all the while being encouraged to sing different music. But they were gospel singers. And gospel is what they would sing. Fast-forward to the 1980s, and they were offered an opportunity that led to astounding crossover success, and to date they've won five Grammy Awards.

I first became aware of them when they performed at one of the early Grammy Awards shows I had attended. Once I learned more about their story, I was an instant fan. Fast-forward a decade, and I was introduced to them and offered the opportunity to discuss telling their story. I couldn't say yes fast enough! But once I got further into the discussion, I learned there was already a deal in place, and it had just been extended for one more year. When an idea won't leave me alone, I know it's because I'm the person to make it happen. So I kept working on it behind the scenes, planning, and waiting for that deal to expire.

It took more than a year of unwavering persistence, and I'm proud to say that my documentary of *The Blind Boys of Alabama* is currently in production.

The journey of *The Blind Boys of Alabama* is a testament to the power of resilience and staying true to the dream you've been given, even when the world tries to steer you in a different direction. Every no we encounter isn't always a hard stop; sometimes it's simply a "not yet." Timing matters, and so does persistence. When the world says no, it might be testing how deeply you believe in your purpose, how willing you are to wait, and how committed you are to knocking on every door until the right one opens. The key is to trust the process, hold your vision, and understand that sometimes the greatest opportunities lie just on the other side of patience.

BE USEFUL ON YOUR WAY TO BEING UNSTOPPABLE

Sometimes even a polite no can feel like rejection. It's natural to want to pull back or even give up. But here's the truth: Being told no is often an opportunity to lean in, stay consistent, and prove your value over time. And the best way to do that is to be genuinely useful to the people you want to work with.

In acting they say, "Don't break character." That same principle applies in life. If your character is generous, helpful, and persistent, then stay that way—even after hearing no. True character isn't just what you show when you're being celebrated; it's what you show when you're being tested.

Years ago I met Lisa Nichols at CEO Space near Lake Tahoe. She was the speaker, and I was just starting out, wide-eyed and eager. I admired her work and dreamed of collaborating with her someday. I even waited in line to meet her and gave her a copy of my first book, which I'd just finished. Over the years, I found myself working with big names in her sphere—Brian Tracy, Jack Canfield, and others—taking on exciting projects and building credibility. But when it came to Lisa, the answer was always the same: no.

It wasn't that she didn't see my potential. It wasn't personal at all. She later told me that she'd been burned before by trusting the wrong people, so she wasn't quick to let new collaborators into her world. I didn't take it personally. I stayed in character. I stayed kind and as useful as I could be to her.

When I began working on a documentary with Giovanni Marsico called *Dreamer*, I immediately thought of Lisa. The film celebrated people who dared to dream big, even when the world told them to keep their feet on the ground. Lisa's story was perfect. I kept asking and kept working to find the right combination of value that would make it worth her time. It wasn't just about me— it was about crafting a win-win.

Eventually she said yes.

That yes turned into coauthoring multiple books together. It even turned into the opportunity for me to produce and direct her one-woman Broadway show—another yes.

Here's the lesson: Trust isn't given; it's earned. Being useful to someone isn't about manipulation; it's about alignment. It's about showing them that you're not just another person asking for their time or attention but someone who brings real value to the table.

So ask yourself this: "How can I be useful while I wait? How can I stay in character, even when it feels as if the door isn't opening?" Every no brings you closer to the yes you're meant to receive—if you stay the course.

Dream On

For many reasons I shouldn't be counted among the best song-writers. I didn't follow the traditional path. Sure, I loved music and gave it a shot in college, but then I took what felt like the practical route—I went to law school, managed bands, and built a successful agency. Songwriting? That was a dream that seemed neither practical nor responsible.

But here's the thing about dreams: They don't need permission to be valid. They only need you to make space for them. Even when I wasn't pursuing songwriting as my focus, I held on to it. I kept room in my life for it.

And because I did, I've gone on to have songs recorded by Lee Brice and Darius Rucker and my music has reached millions of people through streaming. No, songwriting isn't the center of my career, but it's still one of my dreams—and it's alive because I didn't let it go.

All your dreams are valid, and they all deserve space in your life. Some will shine in the spotlight, while others will quietly flicker in the background. The point is to not abandon them because someone else doesn't see their worth.

It's OK if others don't support your dreams; they weren't given *your* vision—they were given *theirs*. Sometimes even naysayers offer wisdom if you're open to learning from them. Criticism doesn't have to crush you; it can refine you.

The most successful people in the world hold on to their dreams with respect and courage. Dreams are whispers from the universe, nudging you toward your potential. If you can dream it, you can do it—Disney got that right. But remember, doing it requires persistence, patience, and a belief that your dreams deserve to exist, no matter how improbable they seem.

Here's the truth: If you don't make space for your dreams, no one else will. If I hadn't kept writing, those songs wouldn't exist. If I hadn't chased after stories that touched my heart, our documentaries wouldn't exist.

And if you don't hold on to *your* dreams, the world might never see the magic only you can create. So keep dreaming, keep learning, and keep going.

They might call you crazy, but I'll call you unstoppable!

About Nick

From the slums of Port-au-Prince, Haiti, with special forces raiding a sex trafficking ring and freeing children, to the Virgin Galactic Space Port in Mojave with Sir Richard Branson, twenty-two-time Emmy Award–winning Director-Producer Nick Nanton has become known for telling stories that connect. Why? Because he focuses on the most fascinating subject in the world: *people*. As an award-winning songwriter, storyteller, and best-selling author, Nick has shared his message with millions of people through his documentaries, speeches, blogs, lectures, songs, and best-selling books. Nick's book *StorySelling* hit The Wall Street Journal Best-Seller List and is available on Audible as an audiobook. Nick has directed more than sixty documentaries and a sold-out Broadway Show (garnering forty-three Emmy nominations in multiple regions and twenty-two wins), including:

- *DICKIE V* (ESPN/Disney+)
- *Rudy Ruettiger: The Walk On* (Amazon Prime)
- *The Rebound* (Netflix)
- *Operation Toussaint* (Amazon Prime)

Nick has shared the stage with, coauthored books with, and made films featuring:

- Larry King
- Kathie Lee Gifford
- Hoda Kotb
- Dick Vitale
- Kenny Chesney
- Magic Johnson
- Coach Mike Krzyzewski
- Jack Nicklaus
- Tony Robbins
- Lisa Nichols
- Peter Diamandis
- And many more

Nick specializes in bringing the element of human connection to every viewer, no matter the subject. He is currently directing and hosting the series *In Case You Didn't Know* (season 1 executive produced by Larry King), featuring legends in the worlds of business, entrepreneurship, personal development, technology, and sports.

Nick's first love has always been music. He has been writing songs for more than two decades, and his songs have been aired on radio across the

United States and in Canada. He is currently ranked in the top 10 percent of songwriters in the world. His songs have been recorded by Lee Brice, Darius Rucker, RaeLynn, Joe Bryson, and many more, and have amassed more than three million streams on Spotify, Apple Music, Pandora, and SoundCloud. He received three Gold records in 2018 for his work with the global touring band A Day to Remember.

Nick has written and/or produced songs that have appeared on the following shows or in promotional commercials for:

- the Fox prime-time series *Glee, New Girl, House,* and *Hell's Kitchen*
- the MLB All-Star Game
- ABC Family's hit series *Falcon Beach*
- the CBS prime-time series *Ghost Whisperer* starring Jennifer Love Hewitt

CHAPTER 5

UNSTOPPABLE

My Journey From Darkness to Light

By Teri Stanley Dimon

I was sprawled on the carpet watching TV and basking in the glow of Christmas lights when my father's boot connected with my side, setting off a shooting pain that reverberated through my body.

"Go upstairs," he spat in disgust.

The pain wasn't just physical; it tore through every part of me as my mind scrambled to understand what I had done wrong. Nothing. I had done nothing. Once again, I was punished simply for existing. Tears streamed down my face as I crawled to my feet, the sting of rejection worse than the ache in my side.

I collapsed onto my bed and sobbed. I hated myself. There had to be something wrong with me—something so fundamentally broken that no one even wanted me in the room. I could hear his voice in my mind: "No one will ever love you." It was a refrain he repeated often. Day after day I was both his enemy and his victim.

Nothing I did was good enough. I breathed too loudly or chewed too quickly, and his anger would flare, reducing me to tears with a single word or glance. "Wipe that look off your face," he'd sneer, his disdain as sharp as a blade.

That Christmas eve, after he kicked me and sent me to my room, my mother came, her eyes filled with something I couldn't yet name. Guilt? Regret? "I have something to tell you," she said, her voice trembling.

"The man downstairs is not your father." My real father, she explained, had left when I was just three months old. He had taken me and my older sister away, only to return me and keep my sister.

So here we were. Stuck with a stepdad who resented me for existing and resented my mother for burdening him with a child who wasn't his. Stuck because for a Catholic woman in the Midwest, another divorce was unthinkable. Stuck because fear held her tighter than hope. Stuck because his family had disapproved of him marrying a divorced woman and he did it anyway, instilling a sense of obligation in my mother to stay.

The truth hit me like a slap in the face. The man who tormented me wasn't even my father. Who was I? I could feel myself frantically trying to connect the pieces of my identity. I was shattered, and yet in that same moment, I felt a flicker of something else: understanding. It all made sense now—the cruelty, the neglect, the way I was treated like an outsider in my own family.

It was both a breakdown and a breakthrough.

I was the physical representation of everything he had lost, a daily reminder of a mistake he had made. As I got older, I processed my pain through rebellion. I taunted him, fought back, and became so disruptive that any shred of harmony in the home was completely gone.

In high school I ran away to a friend's house. Her family took me in and took legal guardianship.

The road ahead was uncertain, but one thing was clear: I was more than his cruelty. And somehow I would prove it—to him, to myself, to the world.

And eventually I did!

The Path to Getting Stronger

They say that which doesn't kill you makes you stronger, and I believe that, but what they don't tell you is that first it makes you traumatized.

There are pit stops on the way to stronger, and they include self-doubt, rage, trauma responses, and a complete dismantling of your mind. Only then do you turn the corner and find yourself at strong.

Today, I am the founder of Diamond Essence Healing™, a healing center with a mission to help people transmute adversity into empowered transformation. I know how vitally important this work is because adversity had trained me into thinking I was a horrible, unwanted person. The meaning I gave to adversity threatened to derail my entire life, and it took years of self-discovery to alchemize pain into purpose.

Healing is not a serene and graceful journey. In fact, it often requires a series of initiations that can feel as though the universe is performing some kind of unfair hazing ritual.

I had started learning about mind over matter in high school, and although the seed was planted, I struggled to integrate the principles into my life. The tapes from my early childhood kept playing in my head: "You're not good enough." "Don't bother; no one will love you."

At some point I decided that if I were perfect, I would be lovable. I figured if I was a super-high achiever, every goal I accomplished could stand as evidence that I was worthy.

I got married and graduated college summa cum laude. I had children and decided to be the best mom, the best homemaker, and the best wife. I was active in the schools, was the homeroom mom, attended every PTA meeting, and volunteered to be a Girl Scout leader. I was always asking how I could give more. My husband at the time traveled a lot, which made life lonely. I decided that if I did more, he would want to be home, so I made sure the house and kids were always taken care of, and I never asked for help—until one day I couldn't get out of bed.

At first, I thought it was a blood sugar issue and tried to look for patterns in my eating. It got progressively worse, and eventually, I was totally immobilized. Yet no one seemed to believe me.

"You look fine," they would say.

"Probably just need some sleep."

But our bodies know. This was not a sleep-pattern issue. This was a wake-up call.

My body ached, and my brain played games with me, some days

being totally blank and other days feeding me suicidal thoughts. I turned to my husband for help, and his reply delivered the final blow to our marriage.

"You're faking it," he said with a sneer. "There is no such thing as chronic fatigue syndrome." With that he walked out of the room, making his position clear; I wasn't behaving the way a wife should behave, and it was a massive inconvenience to him.

His response sparked something inside me, and I became fiercely determined to find the cause and the cure. I began a quest that included visits to many doctors and endocrinologists. I went through a brain scan and sleep studies, but nothing yielded an explanation. Eventually, a friend suggested I see an iridologist who read people's eyes. I had never heard of such a thing, but I was desperate.

The iridologist took one look at my eyes and said, "You have adrenal exhaustion." She handed me herbs and supplements and suggested I massively reduce the stress in my life.

Have you ever found yourself exhausted by life? When just the thought of daily life feels insurmountable, your soul is trying to reach you! Our bodies are our messengers. They deliver symptoms as warnings. Many times our physical pain is symbolic of mental and spiritual pain that we need to pay attention to. Our physical symptoms are symptoms of *misalignment*. The next time you feel exhausted, it might be legit, or it might be prompting you to set some boundaries, let some things go, and start honoring the whispers of your soul.

When I found out that my adrenals had shut down, I realized I had been in fight-or-flight mode my entire life, and I just didn't have any fight left in me. It was explained to me that the adrenals would repair themselves after four more years in bed. That wasn't going to work. I was being robbed of life with my children.

It was time to take my life back. Not long after, I met someone who showed me what true love should look like, and I promptly filed for divorce.

Give Yourself Permission to Honor Your Truth

Sometimes the best decisions are not the easiest. Deciding to file for divorce was one of those moments. It was the right thing to do, but the path that followed was anything but smooth sailing. In many ways it was the beginning of a journey that would test my strength, my faith, and my commitment to living my truth.

Eight years after the divorce, I faced yet another setback. My ex-husband wanted to stop paying alimony and child support since the child was living with him at the time. In court the judge acknowledged that my programming degree was obsolete and ruled that I could take a few years to learn a new trade. But what trade?

I knew I wanted to help people, and that desire led me to study Touch for Health Kinesiology, a holistic approach to healing the body, mind, and spirit using muscle testing and the Chinese meridian system. I poured myself into it, but my efforts were met with scorn.

The judge, my ex-husband, and his lawyer dismissed it as a "hobby," not a "real" business. They laughed at me.

When they mocked my aspirations in court, I felt two emotions simultaneously: utter humiliation and fiery grit. How dare they tell me what I could and couldn't do with my life? Who were they to define my worth? Beneath the embarrassment, a spark ignited. I knew in my soul that I was meant to heal and to serve. I wasn't going to let their limited vision of me dictate my path.

I called upon the Creator, my angels, and my guides. I practiced trusting myself, even when the world seemed to be screaming that I was crazy. Slowly this journey led me into new realms. I started with crystals, then mediumship. I began communicating with higher energies. For the first time, I felt a sense of belonging and wholeness, and slowly I gave myself permission to embrace who I truly was. I told my new husband, "This is me. Like it or not, I am here for a purpose." Thankfully, he was supportive. But more importantly, I had finally chosen to love and support *myself*.

Building my business wasn't easy, but it was sacred work. The judge gave me a timeline to get it up and running, and I reminded myself every day: I am at the right place, at the right time, doing exactly what I need to be doing. I learned to see the gift in every challenge, even when I didn't understand it in the moment. Today my business is thriving!

The lesson I've carried from this chapter of my life is this: Trust the truth of who you are. Give yourself permission to own it. The world may not always understand your path, but that doesn't mean it isn't valid. Ask yourself these questions:

- What made you feel weird as a child?
- What makes you feel different or out of place now?
- What about you do you feel is misunderstood?

The answers to these questions are God's clues to your purpose on this earth. Honor them. Believe in them. Your truth holds the key to your power, your abundance, and the life you were born to live!

CIRCUMSTANCES PROVIDE FUEL FOR GROWTH

I once heard that the most healing way to move through life is to believe that everyone you meet is God in disguise.

Imagine if everyone you encountered was sent to teach you a vital lesson.

I once had a spiritual mentor who explained that we are all souls on the same team. Each of us moves through life encountering other souls who are vital to our growth. We are here to help one another evolve. Our souls seek out the antagonists who will help us move toward the highest version of ourselves. My stepfather played his role beautifully. His way of treating me taught me, by contrast, exactly who I wanted to be. His darkness gave way to my light.

I know what it's like to lie in bed and hate yourself, to wonder what is so fundamentally wrong with you. And I know what the flip side feels like—to understand, deeply and fully, that *nothing* is wrong. Our feelings are not caused by the circumstances of our long-lost childhood or even the circumstances of the present. They are shaped by the stories we create about those circumstances and the meanings we assign to them. When we shift those stories, we reclaim our power.

As I look back, I can see that every failure, every loss, was fuel for my journey. The struggles strengthened me, clarified where I needed to go, and revealed the changes I needed to make. They showed me my patterns and how I was perceiving the world.

Today, I understand a deeper truth. All of life supports me. I choose to always look for evidence that confirms this belief. I am more than enough. Everything I do is enough. I exist; therefore, I am enough. I create value. There is nothing I lack. In this moment, I have everything I need.

Even the most painful experiences hold a silver lining, a lesson, and a gift.

So here is what I hope you take away: Don't give up on yourself or your deepest desires. Trust that all of life is supporting you. Understand that there is more going on than you can see. Other people's projections are not the truth of who you are. You have a unique essence within you, and it's OK to be messy, to make mistakes (they are a requirement, not a flaw), and to not know how to move forward. Just keep going, one step at a time.

Remember, what you are going through is not just happening *to* you—it is happening *for* you.

You are enough, exactly as you are, and your unique light is needed in this world. Let that truth guide you forward.

The child who cried herself to sleep on Christmas Eve now stands as a testament to what's possible when we decide to rise. I am proof that our darkest nights can birth our brightest dawns. To anyone reading this who feels lost, broken, or unseen, know this: You are not the pain you've endured; you are the light that refuses to be extinguished.

Honor your truth. Trust your journey. And remember, the universe doesn't make mistakes—you are here for a reason, and your new story begins *today*!

About Teri

Teri Stanley Dimon is a gifted intuitive guide and healer renowned for her ability to connect with individuals at a profound soul level. With a deep understanding of energy patterns and belief systems, Teri empowers her clients to transcend the obstacles that hinder their growth and potential. Her journey into the healing arts began in her teenage years in the suburbs of Chicago, where her innate wisdom and insight first emerged. Since 2015 she has dedicated her professional life to facilitating transformative change, helping countless individuals discover their true selves and embrace a life filled with peace, joy, and limitless possibilities.

Teri's healing philosophy is rooted in the belief that every person has a unique journey aligned with their soul essence. She emphasizes the importance of recognizing that life is a supportive force, allowing for a natural flow of experiences. "We are not defined by our stories but enriched by our myriad experiences," she often shares, highlighting how these experiences reveal the multifaceted nature of our identities.

Her distinctive approach to healing is a harmonious blend of various modalities, including neuro-linguistic programming (NLP), spiritual life coaching, muscle testing, and energy work. Teri collaborates closely with her spiritual team to create a nurturing and safe environment where clients feel truly seen and heard. This supportive space fosters new insights and breakthroughs, enabling individuals to release past limitations and step into their authentic selves.

Teri is deeply passionate about guiding others on their paths to self-discovery and empowerment. She encourages her clients to cultivate self-love and acceptance, inspiring them to manifest positive changes in their lives. Her practice is infused with love and joy, reflecting her commitment to uplifting those she works with.

Outside her professional endeavors, Teri finds solace in nature, where she enjoys the tranquility it offers. She expresses her creativity through various arts and crafts, allowing her artistic side to flourish. Teri cherishes quality time with her husband, Marty, and their beloved Labrador, Max, who bring joy and companionship to her life.

Through her work and personal life, Teri embodies the essence of healing, guiding others to illuminate their paths and embrace the extraordinary potential within themselves.

Learn more at www.DiamondEssenceHealing.com.

CHAPTER 6

THE GIFT OF MANIFESTATION

By Carolyn Bass

The vision is clear and beautiful.

A masterpiece that started as a whisper of possibility begins to take shape. The artist, passionate and intense, cannot predict the result, and can be carried along only by the stirring within, leaning in to her instinct to create and giving reverence to what begs to come forth.

Materials are carefully chosen, angles are considered against light and dark, and each movement is filled with purpose and intention, coaxing what once was just an idea into a tangible work of art.

The painter puts paints to canvas. The bird gathers twigs and shapes them into a home that holds life. The spider weaves its intricate web. The butterfly completes four stages of metamorphosis.

And the human? We *live*.

The species of the creator and the chosen medium may differ, yet the fundamental truths remain the same; a work of art is nothing but a dream until the artist takes ownership of it and shapes it into reality.

Life is our greatest work of art.

Each thought, decision, and dream is a brushstroke, adding color and texture to the unfolding picture. Like any work of art, there are times when the strokes feel chaotic or incomplete. That's part of the beauty—layers upon layers, each one adding depth to our stories and experiences.

To live with intention is to pick up the brush with purpose, to feel the energy of creation flowing through us! It's trusting that even the messy parts belong, that the masterpiece isn't just the end result. It's the act of creating itself. To live fully is to embrace the idea that life isn't something that happens to us but rather something we have the power to shape.

Our journeys begin as sets of ideas and, like any master-piece, require vision, inspiration, and the willingness to trust the wisdom of our hearts.

Even more important, our journeys require the ability to trust that wisdom when everything around us is falling apart.

THINKING OUR DREAMS INTO REALITY

"Cancer."

My life was forever changed the day my mother told me my father was diagnosed with cancer. I was the only child of two loving and wonderful parents, and this was not news I wanted to hear.

Yet somehow the electric charge of that moment passed, and the three of us, determined not to drown in fear, went on with our lives in hope and prayer. It wasn't long after the diagnosis, however, that we learned we'd have to vacate the home we rented. My father, once strong and independent, had become extremely ill and needed constant care. My mother and I were tasked with the heavy burden of finding a place to live and without the input of my father. My mother, a retired registered nurse, held tight to her positive and courageous attitude and even tighter to her faith. Being immersed in that kind of outlook has served me well in life. Yet at that moment, the reality of being displaced weighing heavily on us, I made up my mind I wanted to own a brand-new home in San Francisco, whether or not I got married. I never wanted to be forced to leave a home again.

My father assured me that one day it would come to fruition, his belief walking alongside my mother's advice to be patient and trust God's timing.

God's timing, it turned out, was much longer than mine. Many years later, as I was packing up to move to my brand-new house in San Francisco, I saw a slip of paper, and on it was written, "I have my house." Manifestation, like any work of art, is a test of patience and faith. Our deepest desires sometimes require a prolonged period of incubation as pieces of the puzzle move around just outside our awareness and fall beautifully, artfully, and finally into place.

I had never doubted that moment—that all the pieces of this wonderfully abundant life were being created over time, as though the universe held a paintbrush, sometimes taking years to contemplate a stroke and other times throwing paint around in frenzied readiness! I realized how similar the art of manifestation and the art of creation really are.

You see, there are five stages in the creative process: preparation, incubation, illumination, evaluation, and implementation. Whether you're creating a painting, writing a story, or building a birdhouse, those stages emerge in a sequential flow and transform a seed of an idea into a tangible reality. These stages also beautifully echo the journey of manifestation, which is a process of creating one's own reality. When we manifest, life is our art, and the intelligence of the heart and mind are our mediums.

In stage 1, we clarify what we want, using "I am" statements. The "I am" statements are key because they focus on the present tense and are positive. In stage 2 we believe what we are manifesting is already true and already ours in total faith. In stage 3 we write out and verbalize or visualize our desired achievements in the present tense and follow the breadcrumbs dropped by God. In stage 4 we take inspired action fueled by an unwavering belief that what we want is already unfolding. In stage 5, finally, we thank God, spirits, people, and more for receiving what we manifest.

In both the creative and manifestation processes, the spark begins deep within—a glimmer of an idea or a heartfelt desire. Incubation and alignment ask us to pause, to trust, to let the unseen forces weave their magic. Illumination bursts forth like sunlight breaking through clouds, much like the vivid scenes of visualization that bring our dreams to life. From there the act of refining and creating blends seamlessly with the inspired actions we take to invite our visions into reality. Finally, the joy of implementation is mirrored in the act of receiving—the moment when imagination transforms into something tangible.

Like creating a recipe, we add ingredients, experiences and beliefs and reshape our lives through conscious and unconscious choices. Every ingredient—whether messy incubation or thrilling illumination—is an essential part of the process. In embracing this, we become deliberate creators, turning the raw material of experience into a life imbued with meaning, beauty, and purpose.

I learned over the years that the greatest secret to the art of manifestation is the art of trusting life itself. Every change, no matter how unsettling or painful, is a brushstroke on the canvas of our destiny. When we choose to embrace the ebbs and flow with gratitude and believe that every ending is not a loss but an invitation to a new beginning, we step into the role of cocreators with the universe. In that trust, miracles unfold, dreams take flight, and life reveals its infinite possibilities.

The Gift of Challenge

I worked for more than thirty years in human resources for the University of California, San Francisco, and while I was excited to take early retirement, the change still felt like a loss.

It was July of 2019, and I poured my focus into my next chapter, preparing myself with new plans and thoughts of wonderful things to come. It was my time to shine with my creative abilities, and it was off to a perfect start. In March of 2020, however, it all came to a screeching halt when the pandemic swept through the world. San Francisco was locked down, and suddenly all the possibilities seemed to dwindle and fade, and my "legal soulmate," Alan, and I were isolated from everyone and everything. Our focus shifted from birthing creative projects to surviving.

There were so many unknowns, and people were dying. The

virus caused a dramatic shift. I made up my mind that I would shift with it! I immersed myself in online health events and adopted a plant-based diet. This one simple change had a remarkable impact on my health and well-being and infused a sense of hope and vitality into an otherwise dark season. We began to create vegan no-salt, no-oil, no-sugar (SOS-free) recipes of our own and share them with others, which evolved into a new endeavor we would never have embarked on had COVID not materialized.

It was also during this time that Alan and I started taking voice-over lessons online and Qigong online. We approached this unprecedented time with curiosity, faithfully following the opportunities dropped into our laps like exciting invitations to new parties with new friends! As life slowly made its way back to normal, we continued to lean in to full participation in life, serving our community and learning new things. A short story I wrote will appear in an anthology that will be published, and I was a featured reader of my work at Ruth's Table in San Francisco. I completed my fourth year as a Great Group Reads volunteer with the Women's National Book Association, and I continue to participate in health events and share my knowledge with others.

One of the keys to manifesting a full-bodied, unstoppable life is to trust that within every seemingly negative situation are the seeds of positive outcomes. We weren't manifesting to become plant-based diet experts. Yet how wonderful that we are! God can see much further than we can, and life will drop gifts right into our laps. Those gifts, however, are often disguised as challenges.

Manifestation isn't about rigidly clinging to a single vision; it's about holding that vision close to your heart while staying open to the gifts life has in store, even those we never imagined for ourselves. Often the path to our dreams takes unexpected turns, revealing treasures we didn't know to ask for. When we embrace the unknown with flexibility and faith, we allow life to surprise us in ways that are infinitely richer and more fulfilling than anything we could have planned or imagined.

I invite you to focus on "I can" and stay true to yourself.

Change, wanted or not, is an invitation to broaden your horizons, to live new stories, and maybe even to meet an extraordinary part of yourself you never knew existed.

EMBRACING THE ART OF LIVING

My mother once told me that everyone in the world is important. If we didn't have everybody, we wouldn't have a world. Think about that for a moment. How boring and colorless our world would be if we all were carbon copies of each other and if my dreams were the same as yours.

The world needs our individual passions and purposes to be what they are—a vivid and colorful tapestry of stories, ideas, and creations fueled by heart and held by soul.

Each of us is a brushstroke on the canvas of life, and we can change the picture from dull to vibrant with a dream, a kind word, an act of service, and an acknowledgment of one another's vitally important contributions.

It doesn't matter what is happening around us if we are committed to focusing on solutions—finding them, giving them, being them.

It takes believing that what we want is already in place.

Forming deep and meaningful connections with other people.

Holding tight to our faith in life's layers and seasons.

Expecting to receive the miracles and opportunities life has for us.

Leaping into uncertainty with unwavering faith that our destiny will catch us!

Those are the keys to making life a masterpiece. There is light. There is dark. There are sharp corners and sweeping brushstrokes and epic mysteries.

And at the center is the artist—*you*.

We all are artists, crafting lives with every decision and every bold step forward. To create is to trust the process. It's knowing that every stroke, no matter how small or flawed it may seem, contributes to something far greater. Every day that we wake up is a chance to leverage our creative genius!

The journey isn't linear. There will be seasons when the colors seem muted and the design unclear. The creator within you knows that creation is an act of faith—a willingness to lean in to the unknown, to let your heart guide you, and to believe that a canvas is masked as a challenge waiting for you to manifest, one brush, one stroke at a time.

About Carolyn

Carolyn Bass is a native San Franciscan. She was class valedictorian of her high school and earned a BA in urban studies with emphasis on environment and energy, and graduated magna cum laude from San Francisco State University.

Carolyn modeled for Emporium and competed in a queen contest. She was a regular dancer on KOFY-TV (channel 20) Dance Party in San Francisco.

Carolyn retired from the University of California, San Francisco with over thirty years of service in human resources and was a graduate of the Diversity and Inclusion Certificate Program. She received a UCSF Achievement Award.

She is a ventriloquist, and her puppet's name is Casey.

Carolyn authored an original short story that will be included in an upcoming published anthology. She was a featured writer/reader at Ruth's Table in San Francisco.

Carolyn cocreates vegan no-salt, no-oil, no-sugar (SOS-free) recipes with Alan Wald. Two of their recipes were featured on *Tuesdays with Thomas* with Chef AJ. Carolyn and Alan won first place with their no-bake SOS-free cookie submission.

She enjoys health education, doing Qigong, and taking voice-over classes.

Carolyn is a member of the Women's National Book Association—SF Chapter and a women's book club. She is passionate about her volunteer work as a Great Group Reads reader and with her neighborhood events committee.

A favorite pastime of hers is watching romance movies.

Contact Carolyn at cbvo4you@gmail.com.

CHAPTER 7

UNSTOPPABLE BODY, UNSTOPPABLE LIFE!

By Neera Sanichara, RN

"**M**ommy, wake up," my daughter pleaded as she wiggled my shoulder.

"I want to go to the pool; why won't you wake up?"

I could hear her, but I couldn't respond. It was as though I were trapped in my own body, my mind aware but my mouth and body paralyzed.

Eventually she gave up and went to the pool with her brother and dad without me. A few hours later I was able to sit up and, with a foggy mind and a nagging sense of guilt, began to piece together what had just happened.

It was my daughter's fifth birthday, and we had taken the kids to Disney World. Her excitement had been contagious, her beautiful eyes sparkling as she took in the decorations, the cake, and the presents. It was her day, and I had worked very hard to make sure it was perfect.

I had worked so hard in fact that I felt I deserved a piece of cake. I had grabbed a large slice and upon finishing that began to eat the cake my kids had left on their plates, savoring the sugary sweetness as the kids darted around in the glow of their special day.

But not long after, fatigue had crept in like a heavy storm cloud. I remember chalking it up to the whirlwind of the day and telling my family I just needed to close my eyes for a few minutes. But hours later I was still asleep, and my children could not wake me up.

The disappointment they must have felt paled in comparison

with the disappointment I felt myself when I looked out the window to see darkness, and the realization set in—I had slept through most of my daughter's birthday.

My mind spiraled. "Was it the cake?" I wondered. "Was my body failing me? Was I not metabolizing the sugar?"

I was a nurse, so I knew the exhaustion I felt was abnormal and a sign of something deeper.

Back home, I went to the doctor, desperate for answers, and her words were like a punch to the gut: "You are prediabetic," she said, the words landing like a ton of bricks.

I was stunned and angry. Angry at my body, at my choices, at myself. How could I, a nurse—someone who should know better—let this happen? In my midthirties? But as I sat with that anger, something deeper began to emerge.

That moment was a wake-up call. I vowed to take massive action—not just to reverse my diagnosis but to rewrite the story I'd been telling myself for years.

It wasn't easy. I overhauled my diet, committed to exercise, and focused on my mental health. Day by day, choice by choice, I clawed my way back to health. A year and a half later, I had lost over seventy pounds, but the most important number wasn't on the scale. It was in my blood tests. I was no longer prediabetic.

That journey taught me something I'll carry forever: Transformation isn't just about weight or health—it's about reclaiming your power, one decision at a time.

That day at Disney World I had sat on the edge of the bed in sadness, heartbroken that I had missed a day of magic. It turns out, the magic had touched me after all.

THE MYTH OF COMFORT

From the time I was a young child, I could see the difference between me and the other girls. They were small and thin. I was overweight.

Now, it didn't matter if my BMI was normal and my body

looked like theirs; I saw myself as overweight. I was heavier, not as pretty, and never quite as cool as the other girls. I was a gifted student; I had secured a spot at the best high school in Guyana. There were only 106 spots available for the 16,000-plus students who had taken the standardized test required at that grade level. The excitement of this quickly soured, as I knew no one at this new school, and the challenging environment, coupled with the normal awkwardness that comes with the teenage years, produced emotions in me that I was unequipped to deal with.

I started high school at age twelve and found myself with more independence. My mom would give me money to buy myself food, and I would come home with bags of unhealthy treats and watch TV as I ate away my feelings, not realizing that food would never fill the empty places inside me.

I discovered yo-yo dieting, eating healthy for a few days, only to slip back into the habit of choosing my favorite comfort foods when life felt unmanageable. "Comfort foods" stimulate dopamine and the reward system in your brain, tricking your body into temporarily feeling good, only to send it crashing a few hours later. The catch is that comfort food never leads to feeling comfortable.

The heavier I became, the less desirable I felt, which triggered the need for more dopamine. It was a vicious cycle, and when I finally graduated from high school and eventually from nursing school, adulthood brought a whole new set of challenges.

Work stress, motherhood, marriage, and finances took turns triggering me right out of healthy choices and into the junk-food drawer.

The day my body shut down and I missed my daughter's birthday was both my breaking point and my new beginning. That's what wake-up calls do—they wake us up from a complacent sleep so that we can finally start living again.

Imagine that when you turn sixteen, you're given a car and told that it was the only car you would ever have. For your entire life, this was the only car you could drive. You'd take great pains to care for it. You'd keep it healthy and dent-free and make sure it was inspected each year. You'd take excellent care of it, knowing that if you didn't, the car would shut down and become useless to you.

The reality is we only get one body for this life.

We must do our best to take care of it.

RECONNECT TO YOURSELF

Reconnecting to our core selves is vital to our experience of life.

As a child, you relished your daydreams, held magical visions for your life, and imagined yourself as powerful and creative.

Then, little by little, you realized that those things you thought made you awesome also made you different.

In time, you learned that different was undesirable, so you squashed that version of yourself, shrinking it until it could fit inside the box of expectations others built for you.

I did it too. It's sort of the hero's challenge of adulthood to recognize when it's happening, wade through the swamp of all the things you never wanted, and find your way back to yourself. The best way to make sure you're living in alignment is to get clear on your own values. I had to build a framework for decision-making so that any time I was asked to do something, any choice I had to make could be weighed against this framework.

If it didn't align with my beliefs and the goals I'd set for myself, it was a no. My people-pleasing days led me straight into diabetes, so I made up my mind that being liked and agreeable was not nearly as important as being alive!

My biggest breakthrough came through the realization that I'm not in control of how others respond to me. I'm only responsible for building up my own internal defenses to handle whatever is sent my way.

My kids played a critical role in helping me to maintain my resilience during challenging times. Not only do I want to be healthy for them, but I also want to set a good example for them.

Every setback became an opportunity to recommit. Every small win reminded me of the strength I had buried under years of self-doubt and unhealthy coping mechanisms. Today, I stand healthier, happier, and more present—not just for my children but for myself.

Finding Purpose from Darkness

My career as a nurse has motivated me greatly to change my life-style and lose weight after being diagnosed with prediabetes. I have failed many times with wellness, having gym memberships I never used, trying different diets, and even investing in expensive exercise equipment, some of which is accumulating dust in my garage as I write this.

I've been motivated in the past for sometimes superficial rea-sons such as fitting into a nice dress or looking good in pictures. However, my prediabetes diagnosis lit a fire in me after which there was no going back. You see, as a nurse I have seen the destruction that chronic diseases can have on one's body. For dia-betes the consequences can include poor circulation, vision loss, kidney failure, and even premature death.

Though I've failed many times at weight loss, I stumbled upon something that made all the difference. In my early thirties I had dealt with a lot, including two complicated pregnancies during which I was on bed rest for two and a half months each, diffi-cult relationships, moving to another state, and losing much of the social support I had.

At this point, I realized that trying to control things on the out-side was slowly killing me. I learned that the only thing I can con-trol is what goes on with me on the inside. Mastering my inner landscape through mindfulness, meditation, and cultivating emo-tional intelligence has been the most powerful thing I have ever done. This is because it can be used in all areas to live a more empowered and peaceful life.

When I went on my weight-loss journey this time, I incorpo-rated the mindfulness tools I'd learned to stop the behaviors that were working in opposition to my goals. The truth is, weight loss is simple; eat within a calorie deficit, and your body will burn fat as energy, resulting in weight loss. However, I believe there are many diet and exercise programs out there that will work, if we can actually get ourselves to do the work!

I've experienced the struggles of an overweight child, a teenager, a young adult, and a middle-aged adult, and as a nurse I've also witnessed the health struggles of thousands of patients and the decreased quality of life of those who have chronic conditions related to obesity or unhealthy habits. I have seen the effects of obesity over the entire lifespan of a human either through my own experiences or through the experiences of others. I feel as if my struggles with my weight have led me to finding my purpose. That has inspired me to create a program called Inside Out Weight Loss®, which helps people overcome their challenges with their weight using a holistic approach.

The Five Pillars of Reclaiming Your Health

What if the foundation of a happy life—one overflowing with joy, energy, and clarity—was totally within reach? The truth is that most extraordinary lives are built on simple principles and routine habits that guide our actions, honor our values, and strengthen our resolve.

After years of personal practice and research, I have found five pillars for reclaiming your health.

1. **Get proper nutrition.** Eating a balanced diet containing adequate amounts of protein, carbohydrates, fats, fruits, and vegetables is a simple and achievable place to start. Once you begin to replace negative eating patterns with positive choices, the change is practically immediate.

2. **Abolish negative eating habits.** Have you ever fallen into the trap of eating healthy all day just to eat a whole bag of potato chips while you watch TV

at night? Or you stick to a diet all week but go out to dinner on Friday night and feel as if you have undone all the work you did all week. As a coach I have found that many people are one or two negative habits away from weight-loss success. When you identify, target, and transform these habits into positive ones, you become more confident in your ability to reach your health goals.

3. **Move your body.** Movement is not just for weight loss. The biggest gift of movement is maintaining your mobility and having the best quality of life as you age. A good strategy is to start off slowly, such as walking five to fifteen minutes a day, and building up consistency. After consistency is established, you can add time and get as creative as you wish, maybe trying one of the fun new activities we now have in the world of fitness.

4. **Practice mindfulness.** Cultivating a state of inner peace is vital. This state may be disrupted from time to time with life's situations. However, processing those situations effectively and efficiently and returning to your inner-peace baseline is where the power is. When my inner world was disturbed by outside situations in the past, my default method, which I was unaware of for most of my life, was medicating myself with food. Once we learn how to handle chronic stress, busyness, and triggers, we can process those emotions and work on responding to them with healthy choices.

5. **Stay accountable.** You can't manage what you don't measure. You've got to write down your goals and track progress. It's also smart to be honest with yourself. If you could do it on your own, you would have by now! I asked for accountability and support

from those around me, and my advice is this: Don't wait until you're sick to ask for help! People hesitate to get help when it comes to starting a wellness routine but go to the doctor when they get sick. Get support now to stay healthy!

These five things are the bedrock of vitality and fulfillment, and you can start using them immediately to improve your life.

The question is, Will you?

I know firsthand how hard it is to break a lifelong pattern. I also know that it is 100 percent worth the effort. As I began to make these five pillars a way of life, self-doubt was replaced with confidence, worries about chronic diseases disappeared, and my mind was at peace. Everything about my life changed for the better, and the best part is that it's backed by science. You don't have to wonder if it will work for you.

These principles are *proven*. They are available right now. They are your path to a powerful life!

This isn't just my story; it's an invitation for *you*. You don't have to wait for a wake-up call like mine. The pillars I've shared are your guide to a powerful, fulfilling life, but the most important lesson is this: You are worth it.

Every mindful decision, every act of self-care, every time you choose progress over perfection, you're writing a new story—a story where you lead with confidence, live with vitality, and reconnect to the incredible person you've always been.

About Neera

For over fifteen years Neera Sanichara has been a registered nurse working in acute care, mental health, home health, and case management. As a nurse she takes a holistic approach in providing quality care for her patients, integrating their physical, mental, emotional, and spiritual well-being.

In addition to her nursing degree, she holds a bachelor's degree in psychology. Her own health struggles have also inspired her to become a Certified Wellness Coach to guide others on their health journey. She approaches health as encompassing the whole being, and the physical cannot be separated from the psychological. Her professional background in combination with her own struggles with her weight has led her to develop Inside Out Weight Loss˚, a powerful program that she created after losing over seventy pounds using her signature framework. She also recognizes the importance of exercise and movement and combines this with fun as a certified Zumba instructor.

As a graduate of the Lisa Nichols Certified Transformational Trainer Program, she has mastered the art and science of speaking, coaching, and group facilitating to share her message to inspire others to achieve their optimal level of health and wellness.

As someone passionate about wellness, she loves to help people take control of their health and build the confidence to achieve their health goals.

She volunteers with the Cub Scouts of America as an assistant den leader and loves participating in community events. In her spare time she loves spending time with her family, cooking, traveling, and enjoying nature.

CONNECT WITH NEERA:

- **Website:** www.wellnesswithneera.com
- **Instagram:** @wellness with neera
- **YouTube:** @WellnessWithNeera
- **TikTok:** @wellnesswithneera
- **Facebook:** @Wellness with Neera

CHAPTER 8

UNBREAKABLE SPIRIT

From Abandonment to Unstoppable!

By Dr. Linda R. Taylor

I t was a warm summer night in New York. Suddenly the sound of raised voices sliced through my mother's bedroom, echoing like roaring thunder.

It wasn't the first time I had heard my parents arguing, but something about this time felt different.

Curious, I pressed my ear to the door. Without warning, it slammed open, and my father stormed out, gripping my hand, and we headed down the stairs. Behind us, my mother's voice trembled with urgency, calling me back to her. In that moment, fear and confusion overwhelmed me, and I sat on the staircase, caught between two worlds. Then came the unthinkable. My parents asked me to decide whom I wanted to live with: my mother, whose steady presence anchored my days, or my father, a figure I loved but whose presence in my life had always been like a fleeting shadow I couldn't quite catch. I was seven years old and forced to choose.

Without hesitation I ran back to my beloved mother, throwing myself into her arms, sobbing. The last memory I had of my father for years was the sight of the soles under his shoes as he walked out the door for the last time.

That night shaped the course of my life in ways I couldn't yet comprehend. My father's departure became the lens through which I viewed and analyzed relationships—a constant reminder that vulnerability led only to abandonment. I believed I was unlovable, that I wasn't good enough. For years I carried that fear of abandonment, allowing it to dictate my dysfunctional choices. Because of that experience, I built walls around my heart to shield myself from ever feeling that kind of loss again. If my dad, who loved me, could walk away and never look back, anyone could.

As a result, I abandoned my core values and lowered my standards. I was drawn to familiar patterns rather than making conscious choices that aligned with my true needs and long-term goals. I was trapped on a relentless emotional wheel, doomed to repeat the painful, destructive cycle—selecting the same prototype in partners each time, hoping for a different outcome but only finding myself back in the same heart-wrenching reality.

Many of us silently endure this pain, believing there's no way out, but I'm here to tell you—there is.

BREAKING THE CYCLE

That destructive cycle led me to engage in unfulfilling relationships that were unequally yoked spiritually, yet I voluntarily stayed past the expiration date. There was just something about a tall, dark, and irresistibly sexy man. Oh, how I had a weakness for chocolate!

The day I hit emotional rock bottom was the wake-up call I didn't know I needed. In that moment of despair, I realized I deserved better. Looking back, that breaking point became a turning point, teaching me the power of facing life's toughest moments head-on and finding strength within when everything felt unsteady. True change had to start from within.

So I decided to realign with my core values, embrace my self-worth, and sharpen my critical-thinking skills, empowering myself to break free from the cycle that had held me captive for so long.

Today, I am a Certified Relationship and Divorce Strategist Coach, and CEO of Divorce Think Tank LLC, a transformational life and relationship coaching firm. I specialize in empowering professional women to successfully navigate challenging life events without losing their sanity, financial security, or faith. Whether a client is seeking a strategy to leave a toxic relationship, contemplating divorce, or struggling emotionally post-divorce, I help them realign with their core values, sharpen their critical-thinking skills, and confidently enhance their self-awareness, allowing them to prioritize their emotional well-being, preserve their financial assets, and position themselves for healthy relation-ships with renewed purpose and focus.

FAITH IS MY ANCHOR

The woman I am today is a testament to resilience, but few know the trials I endured to get here. Life tested me in ways I never imagined, pushing me to my limits. Yet through it all my faith became my anchor, guiding me through every storm.

In 1994 I separated from my son's father. With a renewed focus on building a better life, I enrolled in a one-year prerequisite pro-gram at St. John's University. With unwavering determination, I earned a full graduate scholarship to Howard University's presti-gious audiology program.

In August 1995 I embarked on a new chapter, moving from New York to Washington, DC, where I settled on campus with my four-year-old son. I successfully completed my first year, but when his health began to falter, I left the program and moved to Maryland. The following year, he was diagnosed with chronic asthma, suf-fering frequent attacks that left him breathless and frail.

The day I found him clinging to a railing at school, gasping for air, I knew the situation was dire. He was rushed to Children's Hospital by medevac. In that moment, as fear threatened to con-sume me, I turned to the only source of strength I knew: God. Though I was alone, I felt His presence beside me. Over the next year, we endured endless hospital visits, living under the shadow of his condition.

UNSHAKEN: BATTLE BEYOND THE PHYSICAL REALM

As if my struggles weren't heavy enough, I soon discovered that the neighbor who lived in the apartment downstairs practiced witchcraft. Strange powders appeared at my door, a black balloon covered the peephole, and one day a dead bird was left on my patio. Though terrified, I leaned on Isaiah 54:17: "No weapon formed against [me] shall prosper" (NKJV). Her aggressive behavior escalated, and complaints about my son's noise led to threats of eviction. But God gave me wisdom, so I documented everything. One day she banged on my door and physically threatened me, so I called the police.

When the authorities intervened, they uncovered live chickens, birds, and an altar with beads and powdery substances in her apartment. It was infested with fleas, and the living conditions were unsanitary, leading to her immediate eviction. Only then did we realize that the ventilation system connecting our apartments had likely worsened my son's health.

Through it all God sustained me during that traumatic ordeal. I was more determined than ever to protect my son, so I decided I would sacrifice everything and work around the clock to buy us a home. When I had to leave graduate school to care for my son, God opened a door for me as a loan officer, a career I thrived in despite my inexperience. That job became a lifeline, providing financial stability to secure the quality health insurance we so desperately needed. It also gave me the ability to purchase a newly constructed luxury townhome in a golf course community.

There were days when exhaustion threatened to consume me. I juggled before-school care, school, after-school programs, and even after-after care to ensure my son was safe and cared for. But every sacrifice was worth it. Slowly we built a life of emotional and financial freedom. Looking back, I see how God carried us through every valley. This journey taught me that God doesn't just promise to be with us in the storm—He equips us to withstand it.

WHEN GOD SENDS THE RIGHT PEOPLE

Life often presents challenges disguised as lessons. Reflecting back, I see how intricately God orchestrated every step even when I couldn't understand the plan. At one point I worked tirelessly at a job that barely paid $13,000 annually. Realizing something had to change, I researched and received a mortgage brokerage license, thrived in the real estate industry, and bought the home I still reside in today.

Several years later the mortgage crisis wiped out my savings, leaving me with just $232. When my home faced foreclosure multiple times, I relied on faith and strategy. I discovered legal loopholes, learned about mortgage modifications, and temporarily stopped the foreclosure sale on my home by the grace of God.

When I needed a way forward, God sent answers. A chance encounter led to a paralegal job with a law firm, whose pay stubs helped me qualify for mortgage assistance under the government's HAMP program, and my home was saved. We have to learn to recognize and trust God's hand in our lives. When God is at work, you'll often feel a quiet but persistent nudge in your spirit—an intuition that this moment is significant. Pay attention to those feelings. Ask yourself, "How can I step out in faith to embrace this opportunity?"

God's blessings often require action. They may come in the form of a new skill to learn, a difficult conversation, or a chance to connect with someone who will play a pivotal role in your journey. Seize those opportunities. Trust that even when the path seems unclear, He is working out all things for your good.

THE POWER OF INTERNAL VALIDATION

You're probably wondering how I found the inner strength to move forward when life tried to break me. I walked a path few could understand—choosing celibacy and solitude for five years, a decision that left my friends questioning my sanity. But deep down I knew this journey had purpose. While I still had needs and desires, I resisted the pull to lower my standards or seek comfort in fleeting connections.

God was guiding me through something profound. In that stillness, I embraced the power of choosing myself. I trusted my intuition, realigned with my core values, and gained clarity to make better life choices.

When I moved into my home twenty-five years ago, a neighbor across the street caught my attention. She was a news reporter, poised and self-assured—yet she never interacted with the rest of us in the neighborhood.

One day I introduced myself and asked why she kept to herself. She responded with words that would echo in my mind for the rest of my life.

"Linda," she said, "If you ever want to be considered valuable, make yourself less accessible." The more I reflected on her words, the more they resonated. I realized that by protecting my time, space, and energy, I was raising my own standards. There's a fine line between being inaccessible and being disconnected, and I learned to walk it with grace. I simply chose to connect intentionally when and where it truly mattered. In those five years of intentional solitude, I didn't just find peace; I discovered my true self-worth. I no longer chase validation from others or try to fit into a crowd. Instead, I cultivated something far more powerful—an unshakable sense of inner peace. I came to understand that my self-worth isn't tied to anyone else's opinion or approval.

When I stopped relying on external validation, I tapped into a deeper power: my internal compass rooted in my faith and guided by God. Embracing internal validation has shaped me into the woman I am today. I don't look outside myself for approval or fulfillment. I had finally conquered the fear of abandonment. And the truth is, when you find this kind of peace within yourself, you are never truly alone. God is always with you, guiding you and reminding you that you have always been enough just as you are.

THE POWER OF CRITICAL THINKING

Overcoming my challenges revealed a powerful truth: Life is a series of critical decisions, and the quality of those decisions depends on critical thinking, which ultimately determines our paths. Some events and situations in life are within our control, while others are not.

I've learned that when faced with unexpected challenges, relying on critical thinking rather than emotions is the key to navigating life's twists and turns.

I developed a simple, yet transformative, three-question framework. This method has become a cornerstone of not only how I approach my own challenges but also how I guide my coaching clients in navigating theirs. When you find yourself needing to make a tough decision or facing a crisis, ask yourself these three critical questions:

1. **What is the cost of this decision?**
   - Every decision has a price, whether it's measured in time, energy, resources, or emotional well-being.
   - Take an honest inventory of what you'll need to sacrifice or invest.
   - Is it your peace of mind? Your financial stability? Your freedom or time with loved ones?

2. **Am I willing to pay the price?**
   - Once you know the cost, weigh the pros and cons.
   - Ask yourself if the value of the outcome aligns with your core values and what you're putting on the line.

3. **Whom will this decision impact?**
   - Consider the ripple effect your choice will have on others. Who will be affected?

When you work through the questions, you give yourself the space to understand why you're making a choice and what it means in the larger context of your life. Critical thinking is about giving yourself permission to think deeply and act intentionally. By approaching decisions with this framework, you can move forward with clarity and confidence, knowing your choices are aligned with your core values and purpose.

UNSTOPPABLE

What an emotionally traumatic journey I endured—one that shaped this incredible story I now share with you. My experience carried pain, fear, and nuggets of wisdom—life lessons waiting to be uncovered.

As I reflect on my life, I can't help but think back to that staircase at seven years old, overwhelmed and forced to make a difficult choice. It planted the earliest seeds of the strength and resilience I carry today. If I could speak to that little girl, I would tell her this: "The world tried to break you, but you have a fire inside you that cannot be extinguished. You are truly unstoppable!"

If I could leave you with one message, it would be this: Life's struggles aren't random. Stay rooted in faith and true to your core values, and trust that every hardship you endure is shaping a greater story beyond what you can see now.

Faith, grit, and tenacity are the tools God gives us to face life's battles—use them! The moments you feel lost or forgotten, God is planting the seeds of your transformation. Remember, the hardest decisions define who we become. They force us to choose not just between paths but between perspectives—despair and hope, fear and faith.

My tests are now my testimonies! When life tests you, dig for the life lessons. One day you'll look back and see that even the most painful moments had a purpose. You will turn your pain into purpose and your trials into triumphs.

If my story resonated with you and you're struggling emotionally, and ready to break free from destructive cycles, realign with your core values, and develop critical-thinking skills to make better decisions and life choices, I encourage you to connect with me. Join my community for valuable insights on transformation. You too will become *unstoppable*.

About Linda

Dr. Linda R. Taylor is the CEO of Divorce Think Tank LLC, a women-owned transformational life and relationship coaching firm. She's a dynamic speaker, conflict-resolution trainer, certified family and employment law mediator, and relationship and divorce strategist coach with a passion for empowering professionals.

She guides professionals through life's most difficult relationship transitions, while also helping them advocate for their legal rights regarding discriminatory workplace practices based on marital or familial status. She holds a law degree from Tulane University Law School (summa cum laude) and advanced negotiation training from Harvard and Cornell University, equipping her with expertise in conflict resolution and critical decision-making.

With over fifteen years of expertise in divorce preparation services, divorce and custody mediation, and co-parenting coaching, Dr. Taylor has helped countless individuals contemplating divorce, those struggling emotionally after divorce, and unmarried individuals seeking to break free from toxic relationships, work out peaceful resolutions with dignity to preserve the co-parenting relationship, and develop child-centered parenting plans that are in the best interests of the children—saving her clients thousands of dollars from unnecessary attorney fees.

By combining emotional intelligence, conflict resolution, and legal strategy, Dr. Taylor's transformative Relationship Accelerator Coaching Program empowers clients with the tools to realign with their core values, enhance their self-awareness, and develop critical-thinking skills to make better life choices and decisions—to prioritize their emotional well-being, protect their assets, and position themselves to build meaningful relationships.

For insights into navigating healthy relationships, learn more:

- **Web:** www.DivorceThinkTank.com
- **Email:** LindaTaylor@DivorceThinkTank.com
- **LinkedIn:** Dr. Linda R. Taylor, PhD
- **Facebook:** lindataylor.paralegal

CHAPTER 9

UNSHACKLED

The Strength to Stand in My Own Power

———————————

By Kerin M. Cagle

T he cold steel of the barrel was inches from my face.

A loaded gun. One bullet. And his finger on the trigger.

His hands trembled, or maybe it was my heart pounding so hard it sent ripples through my body. The air between us was thick with alcohol, rage, and desperation.

"This is what you're doing to me," he said, voice slurred, eyes wild. "Playing Russian roulette with my life."

I wanted to run, but where? My mind finally knew a truth my heart had been avoiding for years—this wasn't love. This wasn't safety. This wasn't where I was meant to be.

I had spent years making myself small, shrinking to fit into a love that slowly became stagnant and one-sided. I had carried the weight of his pain and failures, mistaking my endurance for love and my self-sacrifice for commitment. I had finally told him that I needed space, and my courage had been met by his gun.

The signs were always there. The first push when I was holding my baby girl, the drunken threats, the way I learned to tiptoe around to keep the peace.

Luckily, he didn't pull the trigger, but in that moment, something inside me woke up—a voice that said with conviction, "You're not meant for this."

I moved forward with the breakup, but more than that, I moved forward with choosing myself. And in the unraveling of everything I thought I knew, I had to ask the hardest question of all:

How did I get here? If I could answer that, I could make sure I never ended up here again.

THE BREAKING AND THE BECOMING

I grew up surrounded by strong, confident women, but I never felt as though I belonged among them. My sister was perfect, in my eyes, excelling at everything while I struggled to keep up, always feeling like an outsider. My father was my biggest supporter, but even his love couldn't keep my insecurity at bay. I felt safest when I stayed silent and faded into the background. Then, one night my silence backfired.

I was a senior in high school and didn't have many close friends, so when a new friend invited me out, I jumped at the chance. When she suggested we sneak off to the French Quarter, I ignored the pit in my stomach and went along.

We met a group of charming older guys who invited us to a party. I hesitated, but my friend insisted it would be fun. The hotel air was stale, but worse than that, the room was empty.

"Where's the party?" I asked, trying to keep my voice steady.

"They'll be here soon," he said, but I knew the truth. No one else was coming. Then he kissed me. I tried to pull away, but he came at me. My body froze.

I couldn't move. Couldn't scream. Couldn't fight back.

Then he shoved me down, and I felt paralyzed.

My friend banged on the door, and in that moment, I found the strength to push him off and get out. I don't even remember getting home, but flashes of the attack bombarded my mind—his weight crushing me, the sound of my own crying, the sharp pain that came when I realized there was no stopping him.

I never told a soul, not even my parents. I packed it away in the darkest corner of my mind, but the scars were deep. I had already been accepted into college, had a dorm waiting and a future mapped out, but suddenly none of it felt right. I stayed close to home instead and attended a local college, where I still never quite fit in. Memories of that night plagued me. I was angry at myself for not fighting harder. In my nastiest internal dialogues, I even wondered if I had *wanted* the attention after years of being quiet and ignored.

And then one night I met a new man. He was handsome, if not a bit brooding, had kids, and was going through a breakup, so it was no wonder I was drawn to him. His issues may have been red flags for someone else, but for me they were a welcome distraction that allowed me to look away from my own scars and from the parts of me that were still in pieces. I poured everything into him. I ignored the warning signs, the drinking, the way he could turn cold in an instant. I convinced myself that love meant endurance.

And then I had my daughter, and the love I felt for her cleared my vision. One night when she was four months old I confronted him about his drinking, and he snapped. He shoved me while I was holding her. I should have left then, but I didn't. I convinced myself that I could handle it, that he had never hit me, so it wasn't that bad.

But when he pointed a loaded gun at me, something inside me cracked open, and I finally walked away. Not just from him, but from the version of me that had believed I wasn't worthy of more.

My entire life began to change once I chose myself. I started dating a wonderful man, who is now my husband, and I launched my own company called sYmply The Best™. My mission with sYmply The Best™ is to provide a safe, transformative space for women who have experienced similar challenges, to help them find their voices, heal from their trauma, and build powerful lives. I wanted to create what I needed but didn't have during my darkest times. I've made healing and self-discovery a nonnegotiable way of life! Every Sunday, my husband, Rusty, and I sit down to a ritual in which we reflect, refocus, and redirect.

We reflect on what we stand for, what's working, and what's not. We refocus our vision on what truly matters, and redirect our energy to align our actions with our purpose and seek extraordinary opportunities for growth. They are just three simple steps, but they have the power to transform everything. Because healing isn't just about leaving the past behind—it's about learning from it, reshaping it, and using it as fuel to create something greater. The practice of reflecting, refocusing, and redirecting is a road map to discovering your truth, reclaiming your power, and ultimately building the life you were meant to live.

REFLECT ON YOUR TRUTH

What do you stand for? What qualities do you cherish? What kind of life are you building? Not only does knowing the answers to these questions provide a decision-making framework, but it reveals who is meant to be in your world.

Taking time to reflect on your values is like adjusting a compass. When you know your true north, it becomes clear who is walking in the same direction. You begin to recognize the people whose presence strengthens your foundation, whose integrity aligns with yours, whose kindness, ambition, or resilience speaks the same language as your own.

My father was the only person who consistently made me feel worthy. His unwavering support showed me what it felt like to be truly valued. Losing him was devastating, but it also inspired me to become my own advocate and to provide that kind of support to other women through my business. My husband, Rusty, has been equally influential but in a different way. While my father was my rock, Rusty has become my root system. He opened my eyes to the damaging effects I was allowing trauma to create in my life. He challenged me to confront my pain and to break free from the patterns that held me back.

For so long I compared myself with others, retreating into the corner when I didn't feel good enough. Rusty lovingly let me know that kind of insecurity wasn't exhausting just for me but for him. The reality that I could damage the connection we had if I didn't heal was the wake-up call I needed to go all in on choosing myself. I started listening to meditations on my phone—guided exercise to cultivate self-love and peace within. I took time to get clear on what really mattered to me. It was jarring! For so long I focused on others to avoid having to know myself. This stripping away of the distractions held up a giant mirror I was forced to look into.

To my surprise I started to like what I saw. I started feeling connected to my own soul and to others in a way I'd blocked for decades. I started getting familiar with myself and finally became fluent in the language of my inner voice. The more layers of the past I shed, the more deeply Rusty and I fell in love.

This journey is, at its core, a love story—with *yourself*. It's about recognizing that you are not just the sum of what has happened to you in the past—you are the architect of what happens *next*.

Loving yourself means *knowing* yourself, and for that you've got to ask tough questions: "Are the people around me lifting me up or holding me back? Do our values align, or am I shrinking myself to fit? Am I showing up for myself in the same way I long for others to show up for me?"

When you build a life rooted in truth—your truth—you don't just find the right people, you *become* the right person. And that, more than anything, is the foundation of a love story worth living.

Refocusing on What Matters

For much of my life I saw the world through the lens of *not enough*. For so long I focused on the past and on everything that was wrong with my reality. But life has a way of teaching us what truly matters. And my greatest lesson has come from caring for my mother as she battles Alzheimer's.

There are no words for the pain of watching someone slip away while still physically present. Some days the grief is unbearable. But through this experience I have learned that love isn't just about easy moments. It's about showing up when it's hard and finding beauty in what remains. It's about embracing the fleeting, tender moments and realizing that *this* is life—not what's over or what has been lost but what is still *here*.

More than ever I understand the power of being radically present. It's in the way my mother's eyes light up for just a second when she finds something funny. It's in the warmth of her hand in mine. It's in the laughter I share with my husband over coffee, in the incredible bond I have with my daughter, and in the small, sacred joys of everyday life such as watching my grandsons grow. And that has been key to my resilience. Finding moments of beauty, however small. Choosing connection. Staying present, even when it would be easier to turn away.

If everything in your life was stripped away—your job, your achievements, your to-do lists—what would still *matter*? What would you miss? Do you notice the warmth of the sun on your skin? The way a loved one smiles when they see you? The quiet peace in a deep breath?

In the end life isn't measured by what we've lost or what we're striving for—it's made up of the moments we *fully live*.

REDIRECT THROUGH PURPOSE

Not all pain is useless. Sometimes pain informs our purpose. The very wounds we carry hold a clue to the work we're meant to do in this world. I spent so long feeling unseen and unheard that I became the kind of listener I once needed.

This is how purpose often reveals itself—in the places where we need healing the most. I named my business sYmply The Best™ because I believe women are exactly that—strong, yet fragile; powerful, yet graceful; resilient beyond measure. I spelled it with a *Y* to symbolize the journey of finding our *why* as we walk forward in faith.

Purpose has a way of making itself known. As Rusty and I built our financial services business, we realized that money is not just numbers on a balance sheet—it's a tool for impact. That's why we started the 100-Year IMPACT™, working with families, couples, and organizations to shape the legacy they want to leave. It's about more than wealth; it's about meaning. What do you want your life to stand for? What will remain after you're gone? For years I thought I had no mission. But when I followed the small invitations—conversations, moments of growth, new connections—I realized that purpose isn't something you find. It's something you *choose* one step at a time.

You don't have to have your whole purpose figured out today. You just need the *next breadcrumb*. Ask yourself:

- What experiences have shaped me the most? How have they equipped me to serve others?
- Where have I felt the most unseen and hurt? Could that be the place I'm meant to create healing?
- What am I naturally drawn to—what conversations, topics, and causes light me up?
- What do I want to leave behind?

Trust the nudges. Follow the breadcrumbs. Every step you take in alignment with your truth is a step toward the impact you were born to make.

The woman whose silence led to her staring down the barrel of a gun is now just a memory. The young woman who was violated no longer occupies the front of my identity. They are parts of me, but they don't define me. I'm still evolving, but today, I see myself for who I truly am—a strong leader, a woman of resilience, someone who has completely rewritten her story.

And if there's one thing I hope to impart, it's this: No matter what you've been through, you are worthy of healing, connection, and joy *today*. You have the power to redirect your life, step out of the shadows, and create a future filled with meaning and purpose.

Healing doesn't mean erasing the past—it means honoring all of yourself. It means allowing yourself to feel, grieve, express, and be vulnerable. It means asking yourself, "Am I responding as my old, unhealed self, or as the person I am becoming?" It's learning to redirect the thoughts that keep you small, refocus on what matters, and embrace the gifts that have always been within you.

Your journey is yours to shape. Your impact is yours to define. It is my hope that you will look in the mirror and see a brave and bright soul moving forward—because you are *symply* the best—unstoppable, unshakable, and courageous. I invite you to stand tall, own your brilliance, and step boldly into the life you were meant to live.

About Kerin

Kerin M. Cagle is an advocate for empowering women to unlock their unique strengths and rise into their full potential. She believes that within every woman is a story waiting to be unlocked and a strength waiting to be unleashed. She transformed her belief into action by founding sYmply The Best™ in 2024, a transformative space where women are empowered to overcome trauma, break free from limiting beliefs, and forge deep connections with themselves and others, enabling them to live exceptional lives. Kerin's vision is to inspire women through empowerment, self-discovery, and community to rewrite their narratives, step into their full potential, and create lasting legacies for themselves and future generations.

In her professional role Kerin serves as chief branding and strategy officer and co-owner of ASE *Private* Wealth™, a multimillion-dollar firm specializing in strategic financial solutions for high-income earners and private business owners. She's instrumental in shaping ASE's vision, brand, and client messaging to reflect the company's core values of collaboration, advocacy, and meaningful impact on future generations.

Kerin is also co-owner of the *100-Year IMPACT*™ with her husband, Devery "Rusty" Cagle, CEO and founder of ASE *Private* Wealth™ and best-selling author of *Empathy and Understanding in Business*, coauthored with Chris Voss. Together they guide private business owners, high-networth individuals and families, and nonprofits to design meaningful legacies that drive charitable impact on both local and global scales.

Additionally, Kerin is a producer with Abundance Studios®, a cause-based film studio dedicated to creating impactful, socially conscious films that address pressing societal issues while inspiring and uplifting audiences. And soon she'll be adding author to her list of accomplishments, as she collaborates on a new book with the iconic Lisa Nichols, *Unstoppable: Stories of Grit, Determination, and Perseverance*, set to release in the summer of 2025.

Kerin was born and raised in New Orleans. Hurricane Katrina marked a turning point in her life, leading her to rebuild and plant new roots in Greenville, South Carolina. She's embraced this vibrant community with open arms and a resilient spirit. When she's not making an impact in her professional world, Kerin is strength training; focusing on nutrition; diving into books that fuel personal, professional, and spiritual growth; or savoring time with family and friends. She and her husband share a commitment to health, growth, and building a meaningful legacy together. For her, life is about fueling both body and soul.

CHAPTER 10

FIVE MASTER KEYS TO UNLOCKING UNSTOPPABLE RESILIENCE

By Dr. Adrian D. Ware

Than Saturday, I did not bother getting out of bed.

The weight on me felt like the end of a long journey, and I was unsure if there was any road left to travel. It felt as if an elephant were sitting on my chest, squeezing the breath from my lungs. My light had gone out. I had already composed the conclusion to my story in my mind. It was over. I sensed it in every fiber of my being. Deep down I believed the world had already turned its back on me. My life was winding down—slipping away quietly, without a fight.

On Sunday I woke up early and walked into the bathroom, gazing at my reflection. I barely recognized the person looking back at me. This was not the version of myself I had envisioned. The stranger staring back appeared hollow, weary, and broken. I recalled the sink where I brushed my teeth and the cold water splashing against my face. I stepped into the shower. As everything unfolded, it felt as if my life were a slow-motion movie. Time dragged on. My body moved, but my mind felt drained.

As was my tradition, I dressed for my final occasion—a Sunday morning church service. I had thoroughly cleaned my car. I wore a suit, a crisp white dress shirt, a tie, and impeccably polished shoes. I applied my best cologne. I needed to look the part. But inside I was drowning, suffocating under the burden of my own despair. I could barely hold it together. Still, I had to appear as if everything was fine. I had to be perfect.

Hopelessness and despair had utterly engulfed me. Tears streamed down my face. I wiped them away just a few miles from the church. I played uplifting music, hoping to clear the fog in my mind. I was convinced I was heading toward eternity—a quiet, peaceful end to a life that already felt lost. I could almost envision my funeral as I drove up to the worship facility. I had selected the songs the choir would sing and the suit I would wear. My family would know precisely what to do. I had meticulously planned every detail of my memorial.

Entering the church felt like stepping into my final moments. Each step and every breath became a countdown. People chatted while children played joyfully around them. No one noticed my pain. To them I was the intelligent, successful guy who had it all figured out. But inside I was fading away. Families rushed past me, and I floated through the crowd like a ghost. Everything felt distant and muffled, as if I were submerged underwater. The noise, chatter, and laughter sounded muted, as if they were far away. I walked into Sunday school. Then, something unexpected happened.

THE BACKSTORY

I was born in a quiet Mississippi Delta town known for cotton fields, catfish, family, and good food. Memoirs of the King of the Blues, B. B. King, were familiar sights and sounds. King and I come from the same hometown.

Fortunately, I was reared in a two-parent family where I was loved, cherished, and supported. God, family, church, education, and community formed the five pillars of my life. I always believed I was destined to make an impact on the world. My parents believed in me and provided all the tools I needed to leave my mark on this planet. However, my natural inclination has always been toward introversion.

At a young age I surrendered my life to God. This spiritual encounter left an indelible imprint. From that day forward the influence of the supernatural and the Word of God dominated my thoughts. In dreams and spiritual encounters I saw myself speaking to thousands. I envisioned speaking on a platform that appeared to be on a soccer field. People were standing as far as I could see. I connected with thousands of people with life-giving words of life and hope.

There was only one challenge: I was a severe stutterer. When my stammer was at its worst, my head, shoulders, and entire body would shake and twitch as I struggled to speak. It would sometimes take five minutes to articulate one word. The thought of talking to anyone was terrifying. Hearing the telephone ring caused me to break out into a cold sweat.

As a junior pursuing a chemistry degree, my mind began to struggle with my human spirit. My dream was to become a physician, specifically a psychiatrist. I have always been intrigued by the mysterious, limitless power of the mind—a desire I had nurtured since first grade.

My real job would be practicing medicine. I would teach and share spiritual and inspirational concepts on weekends or whenever the opportunity arose. But the call to nurture, soothe, and heal the souls of others nagged me. It would not go away or leave me alone. For the first time, I experienced parts of my being warring and in violent conflict with each other. I was hopelessly fragmented and suffered physical and emotional depletion. Even in my sleep that inner battle continued, draining all my energy. It was tearing me apart. Because of this unrelenting conflict, I could not see where my life was going. My vision went black. The inner battle became so intense that I sank into deep depression.

I found myself on the brink of suicide while in a community with no real answers for me. That same community thought counselors, psychologists, psychiatrists, and mental health care were only for the unstable. No one's arms seemed long enough to pull me out of the Grand Canyon-sized hole where I found myself. By all appearances I was alone. *Depression is its own personal hell.*

One day I concluded I had had enough. It appeared life was not worth the severity of the deep pain I was suffering. Why would God call me to a life of speaking when I could not talk? I could not get a firm grip on how I would fulfill my divine purpose. My life was out of control. I could not take it anymore.

A few weeks earlier I had purchased some cough syrup and Tylenol for a cold that seemed to be creeping up on me. In my mind I heard the words "If you take both of those bottles of medication, it will all be over. Your pain will end. Your life will only be a huge disappointment. You can bring this to an end now and end everyone's suffering. The world will be better off without you."

My belief system was programmed to accept that God was first in the five pillars of my life. Though weighed down as low as ever, I desperately prayed to the all-knowing, all-powerful God within. Deep within my innermost being, I heard these words: "Go to church one last time." *I am not suggesting this is what you must do. The purpose of this chapter is to recount my story.*

The instruction to go to church "one last time" made sense because I had given myself to God and the church. I could not imagine leaving the planet and not returning one last time to partake in what I considered sacred. It would have been my final experience worshipping God on this side of heaven.

I was part of a large congregation. Cars were everywhere, and families hurried to get to classes. *As I walked into Sunday school, everything felt as if it were still in slow motion.* My teacher announced that she would deviate from the printed lesson. At that moment, I sensed that the Holy Spirit had sent me to that class because *He* had prepared a message that would put my life on a path of hope and transformation.

As the lesson emanated from God, I knew it was for me. Her words arrested the work of the darkness that had almost overtaken me as she taught from Genesis 12:1–3. My teacher emphasized the legitimacy of our Christian status with Abraham, his walk of faith, and the inheritance he possessed due to his obedience. I learned that when I received the blood of Jesus through salvation, I was made new—a creation that never existed before. "Therefore being justified by faith, we have peace with God" (Romans 5:1, KJV). Peace! That was what I so desperately needed—peace!

Those words snatched me from the morbid hold of my darkest night. I could now breathe and reconnect with ancient truth, the script of God's mind, the Bible. It became my trusted life jacket. Those words became as warm oil poured into the broken places of my soul. While I knew that complete healing was a distance away, the mending of my soul began immediately. I drove home thinking, "I can make it." I was not out of the woods yet, but I realized the all-wise God of the universe had a purpose and a plan for my life. *God heard my inner cries.* With that understanding, I had the power to take the reins of life, possess it, and walk in it with the anticipation of joy and purpose.

A few days later I was in the chemistry lab, where an acquaintance casually told me she had been studying some faith principles that were transforming her. She had no clue what I had just narrowly escaped. I was hungry for truth that would heal me, then strengthen and propel me into wholeness and fulfillment. As she spoke, I absorbed the information like a man who had not eaten for days.

My current belief systems had proved ineffective, bringing me to the brink of defeat and despair. Eagerly I began studying the Word through the *lens of faith,* allowing it to fill and complete me. I explored its principles and uncovered the truths I had been missing. Healing surged within me, bringing clarity to my life. I learned to meditate on these powerful truths, gaining the strength and determination to navigate desperate, painful, and dark times. I discovered viable pathways to nourish my soul. Over the next nine months, I uncovered these five master keys to unlocking a life of unstoppable resilience. These keys can do the same for you!

FIVE MASTER KEYS TO UNLOCKING UNSTOPPABLE RESILIENCE

Once activated, these five master keys will act together to catapult you into destiny!

1. **Words:** Words formed the foundation of how the world came into being. "By faith we understand that the worlds were framed by the word of God, so that the things which are seen were not made of things which are [currently] visible" (Hebrews 11:3, NKJV). Your life is your "world." You have the power to create the world you desire.

   In a restaurant one of the first things your server asks is, "May I take your order?" What you say determines if you dine well and end the meal satisfied or if you leave dissatisfied. Your voice is the only vote with genuine authority in your life's scenario. Your words seal the deal—for your benefit or detriment. Since the world originated via the release of words, the Earth is voice activated. If we properly use words, they form images, thoughts, and belief systems.

2. **Images:** An image is the next stage of the progression of any word. It visually represents a specific word. A picture forms a unique graphic design within the mind of a thinker. *Webster's Dictionary* (1828 edition) says an image is "the likeness of any thing on canvas." It could be a picture, a resemblance painted, any copy representation, a show, an appearance, an idea, a conception, or a visual image.

   Visualizing yourself in these images allows your soul to visit your future and propel you toward your highest potential. An image transcends the concept of words. It elevates to the level of a symbol or a representation that embodies words—whether spoken or imagined. As you embark on a path to wellness, it will be crucial to hold on to images of your future to remind yourself of the life you aspire to create. Visions of your ideal life etched into the subconscious will replace old memories from which you are moving away and distancing yourself.

3. **Thoughts:** Thought is "a developed intention or plan."[1] The word *thought* comes from an old English word meaning "to devise or to plan," "to ponder," or "to contemplate."

   Thoughts are an organized (or disorganized) arrangement of animated images formed from words. While images represent still pictures, thoughts are akin to videos. They arise from spontaneous or deliberate processing of words, images, concepts, or ideas. Intentionally choosing what you focus on boosts your confidence and empowers you to achieve your highest potential. Treat your brain like a muscle; exercise it to keep it strong and fit.

4. **Belief Systems:** One's belief system is the self-sustaining force that causes the brain to run on autopilot. A deceived or misinformed belief system is often the reason one experiences hopelessness, sinks into chronic depression, or has thoughts of suicide.

   Since belief systems arise from the first three master keys, they profoundly impact the quality and sustainability of one's success. Belief systems can either uniquely unlock the doors to the opportunities you seek or block the paths you wish to avoid.

   Teachings, environments, associations, and experiences shape belief systems. However, one can reprogram the subconscious mind using words, images, thoughts, belief systems, and corresponding actions. Success is not automatic; instead, it occurs by activating the five master keys.

5. **Corresponding Actions:** Corresponding actions involve acting—spirit, soul, and body—in alignment with and complete submission to your belief systems. Corresponding actions are the most natural extensions of true faith. They are faith personified and demonstrate one's true beliefs.

How can you believe something but not act on that information? Imagine you and I were trusted friends and I came across your name in a reputable publication that stated you had nine million dollars in unclaimed funds. To claim those funds, you need to go to your Secretary of State's office with three forms of identification. The Secretary of State's office is only fifteen minutes from your home.

If you somewhat trusted me, you would google the publication and research it for yourself. But if you had confidence in my words alone, you would appear immediately at that Secretary of State's office with three forms of identification in full anticipation of walking away with nine million dollars. Even if you needed to take a few hours from your employment, you would make it happen.

If you did not act on my words, you would have difficulty convincing anyone you trusted me. Even the most affluent person can use nine million dollars. A refusal to act demonstrates doubt. In the same way, if you accept the concepts I share in this book, you will act on their truths.

ENDNOTE

1.   Merriam-Webster, s.v. "thought," accessed March 27, 2025, www.merriam-webster.com/dictionary/thought.

About Adrian

Dr. Adrian D. Ware is a dynamic force in personal transformation. As a pastor, public speaker, ghost-writer, transformational coach, and premarital/marital coach, he has dedicated his life to empowering individuals to reach their fullest potential. With over twenty-five years of experience, Dr. Ware is a trusted, faith-based thought leader who helps people elevate their thinking and actions to achieve lasting success. His coaching inspires profound growth, fosters deeper connections, and facilitates the realization of one's true potential.

He presents universal principles for understanding and healing from the aftermath of trauma, such as depression and setbacks, and discusses how to overcome their grip. Drawing from extensive experience, Dr. Ware identifies that trauma is often so profound that people delineate *time* and *events* as before and after the trauma, marking it as their point of demarcation. Trauma imprints itself on the soul and demands respect for its devastation.

Dr. Ware's relentless pursuit of uncovering core issues makes him an invaluable transformational coach for clients worldwide. His exceptional ability to connect with individuals in crisis stems from his insight that hopelessness has a structure that can be dismantled piece by piece. His philosophy is built on Five Master Keys, which guide individuals away from limiting beliefs and emotional turmoil, empowering them to achieve greatness.

Dr. Ware's journey serves as a powerful testament to his philosophy. Having overcome chronic depression and suicidal thoughts, he assists others in breaking free from their trauma. At the age of twenty-one, he walked back from the brink of suicide, an experience he shares in his upcoming book *How to Go from Trauma to Tremendous*. In this memoir, Dr. Ware demonstrates that overcoming trauma is not a one-time event but an ongoing process. His quest is to teach others to embrace their journey.

Dr. Ware possesses an impressive academic background, including a Bachelor of Science in chemistry, a Master of Business Administration, and a Doctor of Ministry. He combines academic intelligence with spiritual wisdom to create transformative programs that empower individuals to thrive in personal, relational, and spiritual areas. His expertise encompasses crisis management, suicide prevention, and emotional health education. He authored *The Journal of Emotions* and emphasizes holistic well-being.

Dr. Ware enjoys cooking, reading, writing, traveling, spending time with family, and watching law dramas. He and his wife, Tonya, have been happily married for over twenty-nine years and are the proud parents of two daughters, Wisdom and Wealth.

CHAPTER 11

THE SEASON OF SUDDENLY

By Tameika L. Chambers-Pope

A friend of mine once told me that there are actually five seasons, not four: winter, spring, summer, fall, and suddenly. We know when the other four seasons are coming, and as such, we properly prepare. In winter we get our car "winterized," or cover the windows in plastic. For spring we "spring-clean" and plant our flowers. For summer we put screens in the windows and try on last year's swimsuits. And for fall we plan our Halloween costumes and decide who will host Thanksgiving dinner.

For the season of suddenly, however, we find ourselves unprepared. Suddenly doesn't ease in with changes in colors and temperatures. No. Suddenly delights in shocking our systems. Sometimes suddenly brings miracles we never could have predicted or heartache we never saw coming. Often, tricky as she is, she brings both, in quick succession, trapping us in a back-and-forth dance between anguish and gratitude. In whatever she brings, she's calling us to step into a new layer of self-awareness, a new level of self-actualization, a potential we didn't know we were capable of.

Now, because we don't partake in some annual routine as we do for other seasons, we feel blindsided when something we didn't expect suddenly enters our reality. What I now know to be true is that we absolutely *have* been preparing for suddenly. With seeds planted over the years, and strategically placed in various parts of our journey to pull from as needed, we were being primed for suddenly to make her appearance.

The secret is to remember where to look for those seeds when suddenly season hits. My biggest moments of growth have all occurred during suddenly season.

The first suddenly season occurred in primary school when I decided to join the school play. The production was *Fame*—a show I adored. I figured I'd be an extra—just a quick kick-ball change in the background, and off the stage I would go. Simple.

But suddenly I was choreographing the main number, leading the dance, and singing the theme song! My family's shocked faces in the audience said it all. They had no idea I was the lead. Honestly, neither did I! One moment I was imagining myself in the wings, and the next, I was front and center, in a space I hadn't planned for, terrified, yet exhilarated. That was my first taste of suddenly. Life swept me into something unexpected and extraordinary, inviting me to express my brilliance in ways I never thought possible.

But suddenly doesn't always wear sequins.

It wasn't long after my time in the spotlight that she showed up wearing a much different costume. This time suddenly reared her head in the ugliest of ways that would change the trajectory of my life forever. Sometimes through the use of another person suddenly decides the next lesson at hand. This was the case when she decided the predator my mom was dating would be the best vessel to carry out her wrath.

I was in middle school and had just gotten my hair silk pressed. The stylist suggested I sleep on a satin pillowcase, and my mother's boyfriend had one.

I was familiar with him. I never liked him, but I'd been to his house before, so I was comfortable going to get the pillowcase. He answered the door and told me to come upstairs.

Suddenly he said, "You can't have the pillowcase for free. I'mma need a kiss."

When I said no, he grabbed me and kissed me, shoving his tongue into my mouth as I struggled to turn my head. I pulled away, darted for the door, and ran home. I didn't cry. Shock prevented any tears from flowing. When I finally told my mother, she gave me a hug and said she would deal with this. I was so relieved. Finally, this man would be out of our lives. Or so I thought.

When she confronted him, he told her I was lying, and somehow he eventually moved into our home. I felt betrayed and abandoned, and my relationship with my mother became estranged. Weirdly, I didn't feel unsafe around him because I'd already decided that if he tried anything again, I would defend myself in any way necessary. He didn't, but still things got worse. One day my mom and I got into an argument about him, and I left the house for the night to cool off. I didn't tell her where I was going, so in her mind I had run away. I guess in a sense I had. I called her the next day, and we agreed that I'd come home to talk things out. When I got home, I unlocked the front door, and my mother was standing there. Calmly, she said, "Give me your key." I obliged. She then said, "Take a few steps back." I was confused, but I slowly started backing out onto the front porch. Once I was just outside the door, she closed it and locked it without a word.

Suddenly I was sixteen and homeless.

THE SEED OF UNSTOPPABLE

If you ask a hundred people what it means to be unstoppable, you'll likely get one hundred similar responses, all having to do with never giving up.

When I became homeless (albeit for a short time, as my cousin took me in that same day), I didn't feel unstoppable. I definitely stopped. Stopped and cried. Stopped and mourned the loss of the fantasy of the relationship I was supposed to have with my mother. Stopped and panicked about what would happen to me. But then I did something else. I rebelled. At the time, of course, I didn't realize that *rebellious* and *unstoppable* were synonyms. I now know that one can't exist without the other.

I didn't rebel in the sense that I started getting into trouble. I rebelled against anything trying to steal my happiness. I rebelled against the notion that I wasn't good enough and would never rise from this adversity. I rebelled against my wounded ego that kept me angry at my mom.

And little by little I healed. I'd fall, I'd learn, I'd grow, and then I'd rinse and repeat until the lessons became clearer and easier to comprehend and accept.

Moments of suddenly can feel like lightning bolts splitting the sky, dividing life into before-and-after moments, but if we can learn to partner with sudden change instead of fighting it, the seed of unstoppable begins to grow.

As I began to realize that the sudden status of homeless hadn't killed me, I renegotiated my relationship with suddenly. Eventually the pain I felt forged a fire of resilience within me. I saw my struggle not as an ending but as motivation to begin again. Each scar became a source of pride, evidence that I was not broken but reshaped and resilient.

No one is born unstoppable, and that's great news because it means you can learn to cultivate the three habits that awaken the unstoppable warrior within: empathy, purpose, and faith.

Unstoppable Empathy

As you can imagine, when my mother put me out, I became angry. That day, I moved in with my cousin and vowed to never speak to my mother again. As I sought therapy, however, I realized that my mother was not just my mother. She was a human being and as such came with her own set of triggers, trauma, and beliefs based on her own experiences.

As I learned to see her as a separate being, I realized she was bringing to the table a lifetime of her own lessons and doing the best she could with the awareness she had. None of these revelations happened overnight, and eventually she did leave this horrible man.

Seeking to understand healed me and in time repaired my relationship with my mother. I couldn't heal while simultaneously blaming her. This was about me and my fortitude, not about my mother and her choices. She had a journey separate from mine.

Empathy is a cord that connects us to the experiences of others. It's in seeking to understand, rather than to win, that damage is repaired, bonds are formed, and love can again take root.

Unstoppable Purpose

I studied journalism in college. My goal was to be the next Oprah, and I was well on my way. I even secured a highly sought-after internship at Black Entertainment Television. Yet when I graduated, I couldn't find a job, so I asked a recruiter friend to review my resume.

"Change your name to Tammy," she said. "None of these companies are looking for a black girl named Tameika."

Shocked and resentful, I re-sent my resume as Tammy to the same places where I'd applied as Tameika, and sure enough, I started to secure job interviews. You might think that made me happy, but I was infuriated.

Suddenly I was on a new career path.

I wasn't going to let this kind of discrimination happen to other people. My goal was to help talented people find good jobs and be treated fairly. Thirty years later I'm still doing it, as head of HR for one of the most influential organizations in the world!

That fire within you—your purpose, your passion—is what makes you unstoppable. Think about moments in your life when you've felt driven by a cause bigger than yourself. Those moments aren't coincidences; they're calling you to step up and create change.

When you find a purpose that sets your soul on fire, it transforms obstacles into opportunities and frustration into fuel. Ask yourself what fire is burning within you and how you will use it to make your mark on the world. That's where your power lies.

UNSTOPPABLE FAITH

For thirty years I believed I had a marriage worthy of the Hall of Fame. It wasn't perfect, but my husband and I had built a life filled with love, laughter, and accomplishments. As the years passed, however, cracks began to form. Resentment crept in, and I carried its weight silently for years, trying to "fix" our marriage with extravagant vacations and public displays of happiness. Yet behind closed doors, we were unraveling.

During the chaos of COVID-19, life became a storm we couldn't weather. We lost ten family members and friends. One of our daughters fell unexpectedly ill, requiring constant trips to The Johns Hopkins Hospital. I was working from home, and my husband, a forensic scientist, was under immense stress—navigating intense workplace pressure and the emotional toll of everything happening around us. I was so overwhelmed that I couldn't see his silent battles, nor did he share them. Then came a devastating revelation—something that broke my trust and shook the foundation of our marriage. After twenty-five years of commitment, I felt betrayed in ways I couldn't even articulate.

Individual therapy and group support became my lifeline, but the scars ran deep. For three years I thought the betrayal was the end of our marriage, but as I dug deeper, I began to understand his, and by default *our*, silent struggles. I learned there had been an intricate web of challenges that had shaped his choices, and unknowingly our relationship, that neither of us was aware of. With this new knowledge I believed we had a chance. He went to therapy as well, and I began to have hope that we could save our marriage. What I didn't know was that he had already begun to emotionally distance from me.

Not long after my ray-of-hope moment, we had a horrible fight that broke us once and for all. The weeks that followed were a haze of grief. I couldn't eat, couldn't get out of bed, couldn't breathe. I was devastated. I watched thirty years of marriage go up in flames in thirty days. There was no last kiss or last try. It was just over, suddenly.

And yet in that darkness I found the light of faith. Exactly one month later I wrote a list of manifestations. Since then I've experienced an extraordinary season of suddenly: unexpected opportunities, new connections, and a deep sense of renewal. My small group of friends became my lifeline, showing up at all hours with unconditional love. My daughters, nineteen and twenty-two, became my reason to rise each day. They were watching, and I wanted to show them what resilience looked like.

Slowly the fire within me rekindled, and I am more alive than I've ever been!

This period of darkness called to mind one of my favorite quotes: "One doesn't have to be perfect to be useful." It's a reminder that imperfection doesn't disqualify us from meaning or purpose. Even in my brokenness I could alchemize the pain into something greater. I leaned in to traveling, new self-care rituals, and heavy prayer and meditation. I allowed myself to fall apart, trusting that destruction makes way for rebirth. Like every season, adversity is temporary.

Faith reminds us not to write the ending prematurely—because sometimes the story has only just begun. We must remind ourselves that darkness is temporary. It's a season, and seasons are impermanent. One day, quite *suddenly*, the sun will start to rise, the grass will turn green again, and you'll come back to life stronger than ever.

Just as the dead of winter gives way to the bright blooms of spring, your pain will eventually melt, and the bud of a new beginning will crack through, reminding you that it's time to grow again, to bend toward the light, and to start the next season.

Unstoppable Growth

Author Paulo Coelho wrote, "When we least expect it, life sets us a challenge to test our courage and willingness to change; at such a moment, there is no point in pretending that nothing has happened or in saying that we are not yet ready. The challenge will not wait."[1]

Each time suddenly knocks on our door, it's an invitation to grow. Each time sudden change hits, we've got to trust that it's not a catastrophe but a divinely timed plan playing out before our eyes, because the universe is always way ahead of us.

We simply must allow ourselves to meet the moment with courage and trust the unfolding, to pretend that the change was our choice and act accordingly. Just like the other seasons, suddenly is here to teach us. It molds us into the version of ourselves we're meant to become. It whispers that the storm is never the end—it's the clearing. It reminds us that every fallen flower enriches the soil, every scar carries a story, and every setback sharpens our resolve.

The season of suddenly manifests transcendence, not simply survival. And when the next suddenly arrives, as it surely will, leaning in to the security that growth is inevitable can foster a sense of peace. The season of suddenly becomes a bridge between who we were and who we are becoming, reminding us that each moment of upheaval is a call to evolve, not to retreat.

ENDNOTE

1. "Paulo Coelho Quotes," Goodreads, accessed March 27, 2025, https://www.goodreads.com/quotes/62867-when-we-least-expect-it-life-sets-us-a-challenge.

About Tameika

Tameika L. Chambers-Pope is a human capital development executive whose thirty-year career spans from Wall Street finance to K Street government and, most recently, to Broadway as a newly minted theater producer. Through her coaching business, Cultivate to Great, Tameika specializes in leading her clients to finding their authentic path to success through mastering self-awareness.

Tameika's expertise has been nationally recognized in *Essence* magazine, *Diversity Woman* magazine, The She-Suite, and Women to Watch Media. Leveraging her degree in communications, her passion for women's empowerment, and her experience as a certified life coach, Tameika is also an inspirational speaker, a writer, an expert panelist, a host, and a board member of the oldest domestic-violence shelter in Washington, DC.

Originally from Annapolis, Maryland, Tameika currently lives in the suburbs of Washington, DC. She enjoys spending time with her two daughters, Chandler and London; traveling; and immersing herself in what she calls "indulgent self-care," which fuels the grit that fosters her dreams.

Learn more:

CultivateToGreat.com

Tameika@CultivatetoGreat.com

CHAPTER 12

FROM TRAUMA AND TERROR TO TRIUMPH

*The Keys to Cultivating Resilience,
Strength, and Perseverance*

By Nancy Wolff

My vision went black as my head slammed hard into the window.

I remember being shocked that the window didn't break, but I didn't have that long to think about it, because the next blow came hard and fast and knocked me to the floor.

I tried to fight back, but my partner put a pillow over my face, pressing down until I couldn't breathe. When he finally removed it, he stuck his hand in my mouth to prevent me from screaming, and I bit down hard, realizing too late that I was not biting his hand but my own tongue. The pain was excruciating.

I scrambled up, threw my suitcase down the stairs, and ran to the car. He beat me to it and got in the driver's seat, promising to take me to my parents. I should have known not to trust the sudden change in dynamic.

He pulled off the highway and drove down a dirt road with a pond at the end of it. Before I could ask what was happening, the cord from the car phone was around my neck.

"I'm going to kill you," he said menacingly through gritted teeth. "I'm going to kill you, and no one will ever find you."

Somehow I managed to press the 911 button, and the cops showed up. They asked if I wanted to press charges, but I caught my partner's eye, and I knew if I did that, it would only get worse. We got in the car and went home, my stomach sick with the knowledge that it would only continue—and it did.

One day he threw a knife at me. Another day he dragged me around my house so forcefully that my robe ripped apart. I don't remember what I did the day he twisted my hand so hard that the bone fractured, but twenty years later I can still feel the pain.

He was a veteran, and when I moved in, I had no idea what I was getting into, no idea that the slightest shift in the tone or volume of a conversation would set him off and unleash a living nightmare.

Dare to Dream

I watched from the window as he pulled the car out of the driveway. I knew he'd be gone for several hours, so it was now or never.

I withdrew $3,000 from my checking account, packed everything I could, and left. You might think it was liberating, but it wasn't. I looked over my shoulder constantly, terrified he would send his policemen friends after me. I paid cash for everything so he couldn't track me. I traveled nine thousand miles in two months. It was exciting at times. I got to see at least twelve different states, and while I'm not sure I ever quite exhaled, a spark was lit within me.

I had done it.

As I drove on the open road, I had a lot of time to think about how I had landed in such a dangerous situation, and it didn't take long to connect the dots. My parents had a long relationship, but they were always fighting. I only saw my father raise his hand to my mother one time, but the mood was often dark and unpredictable. I learned to stay quiet, to endure.

With my partner, when the signs of dysfunction first appeared, I thought they were normal. By the time the abuse began, I felt completely trapped.

It happens to so many people. Our instincts tell us that

something isn't right, but our programming overrides it. I instinctively knew that the way he spoke to me was wrong, but I had grown up hearing it, so I stayed. And stayed. Until the day that staying felt scarier than leaving.

Those months on the road had shown me what freedom tasted like, and yet, like so many other women, I ended up going back. I had come home to visit my parents, and he convinced me to meet him. I agreed but insisted we meet in public. The man who walked into the restaurant was not the angry, seething man I had left, but a humbled, apologetic man seeking to right his wrongs. He gave me a recording of himself begging for forgiveness and promising to never hurt me again. He asked me to give him one month to prove it. And I did.

While the abuse never did get as bad as it had been before, something in me had changed. I had tasted freedom and sovereignty. On the road I had allowed myself to envision a better life, which made this empty loveless one completely intolerable. When he finally met someone else, and I finally made up my mind to live a full life, we ended the relationship once and for all.

You see, during those two months on my own, I had begun to imagine a different life. At first, it was just glimpses—a fleeting picture of peace, safety, and joy. I started to ask myself what it would be like to wake up without the weight of walking on eggshells or to wake up unafraid.

Those questions became the seeds of a vision. It wasn't just about what I wanted to escape; it was about what I wanted to *create*. I knew what despair felt like, and having experienced the contrast, I could use it as a guide to craft something better.

Envisioning a better life doesn't require every detail to be clear at the start. You don't need to know how you'll get there, just that you will. Start by giving yourself permission to dream. Write it down. Speak it aloud. Picture it as vividly as you can—your surroundings, the way you feel, the people you allow into your space. Focus not just on what you want to have but who you want to become.

But vision alone isn't enough. To cultivate it, you must also cultivate yourself. Over the years, I read endlessly—books on self-development, psychology, spirituality, anything that could teach me to think differently and strengthen my resolve. I sought out mentors and adapted their practices into my own life. I meditated, journaled, and challenged my old beliefs. Each step helped me build a mind and spirit capable of not just imagining a better life but *fighting* for it.

Crafting your vision from contrast is a powerful tool. The darkness you've experienced shows you exactly where the light is needed. Write down everything you've experienced that you never want to again, and then write its opposite. My darkest memories gave form to my brightest dreams, and though the road to realizing them was long and bumpy, the journey was worth every step.

Take 100 Percent Responsibility

Have you ever noticed something—a credit card bill getting too high, or a contract that doesn't seem right—and for reasons that make no sense, turned the other cheek?

It's human nature to avoid uncomfortable things, especially when life feels as if it's closing in on you. I know because I let myself be swept into decisions my instincts screamed against. I signed my name to loans and contracts I barely understood, bullied into compliance by someone I thought I could trust. But looking away didn't save me from the consequences; it only magnified them. Like so many of us, I was overwhelmed, clinging to the hope that things weren't as bad as they seemed, even though I knew they probably were. It's a trap we fall into when fear paralyzes us, and the weight of our responsibilities feels too heavy to bear. But the truth is, facing reality is the first step to reclaiming control and building a life of integrity and strength.

I knew I needed guidance—mental, emotional, legal, and financial guidance.

My bad decisions had destroyed my credit, and as you can

imagine, that affected every area of my life and made it difficult to start over.

He forced me to sign for a boat and to buy him a car in my name, as well as add his name to my credit cards.

Other decisions I felt coerced into making further harmed my finances. And the whole time my intuition was screaming at me to protect myself, but the problem was he screamed louder.

When I was slapped with a $3,000 bill from my lawyer that I couldn't pay, I understood why desperate people do desperate things.

That feeling inspired me to become an associate with LegalShield. I knew what it felt like to not have access to top-quality legal advice at an affordable price, and I wanted to help other women avoid the shame I had experienced.

Even if you're not trying to steer your way out of an abusive relationship, the advice to stay hyperaware and responsible is still valid.

Do you know your financial situation? Do you have a will? Who is your accountant? Are your taxes being handled fairly? So often people, and mostly women, fail to look under the hood because the thought of what we might find is overwhelming. I'm here to tell you that it's a lot more overwhelming if you ignore it all until it spins out of control.

My breakup was a huge wake-up call. I threw myself into work, dedicated to improving my financial situation and regaining my confidence and self-esteem. By focusing on small victories, such as improving my credit score so I could refinance the mortgage, I gradually started to rebuild my life. The support of loved ones, as well as a deep inner strength, helped me push through each difficult day.

Ultimately this setback became the catalyst for growth and led to a significant life shift. I had to change my career choice and eventually found my way into the insurance industry.

As I joined a network marketing company that would help educate me and remove derogatory items from my credit reports, I learned of success stories from those who had gone from bankruptcy to millionaires. I met these people and knew if it could happen to them, it could happen to me. It is so important to have the support of people who believe in you more than you believe in yourself. I finally began to see the light as my credit score began to rise. I found out how important financial literacy is and vowed to pay the education forward. I learned it takes seven years to remove loans that are settled for less than the full balance.

It wasn't easy. Imagine working for fourteen years on a business and ending up with nothing except the bills.

Resilience requires awareness, and awareness takes courage! Ask for the help you need.

I am grateful now for that experience. Never again will I look away. Never again will I relinquish responsibility for my own life. Never again will I be the victim of my own ignorance!

DECIDE WHY YOU WERE BORN

I could feel the sun on my face and smell the ocean.

The catch was I was not anywhere near a beach but staring at a wall in my office. I had joined Avon, and the prize for hitting a sales quota and gaining three new recruits was a trip to Atlantis. I was determined to earn that trip.

To me it wouldn't be just a vacation. It would be a testament to what's possible when you shift from seeing yourself as the victim to seeing yourself as the victor. I decided at that moment that this is my destiny.

I was here to show other people that they could defy the odds, dare to envision a better life, and do what it takes to get it.

Deciding why you were born is one of the most liberating choices you can make. In a world that pushes you to *find* your purpose, the pressure can feel unbearable—especially when you're struggling just to see the next step. But what if you don't need to *find* anything? What if you could simply *decide*? *Decide* that you were born to create joy, to bring light into dark places, to show others the way. Purpose isn't something to be discovered—it's something you can declare for yourself. When you make that decision, you give your life meaning, and that meaning becomes your compass.

Once I decided that I was born to be a model of resilience and perseverance, I became more determined than ever. I earned that trip, and I continue to set giant goals, not just for myself but so they could stand as evidence of what is possible!

What about you? What would you like your life to mean? And what will you do next to embody that?

RECLAIM YOUR MIND AND YOUR LIFE!

I once heard a speaker say by changing your words, you change your perspective. Instead of saying, "I'm nervous," I say, "I am energized." Instead of saying, "I'm overwhelmed," I say, "I am in demand!"

Learning to shift my perspective has completely changed my experience of life.

For fourteen years I was manipulated, controlled, and constantly belittled, experiencing physical violence, financial coercion, and deep emotional trauma. Yet for me my greatest accomplishment wasn't escaping physical and emotional abuse but regaining my confidence, self-esteem, and trust in myself.

I've now been married to an incredible man for nineteen years who is my best friend and biggest supporter.

I have a thriving career and have built a fantastic life for myself. None of it would have been possible if I hadn't believed in my vision and followed my dreams.

Reclaiming your life doesn't happen overnight—it's a journey of small, consistent steps that build into monumental change. Focus on getting just 1 percent better every day.

No matter how far you've fallen or how broken you feel, remember this: Every day is a new opportunity to rewrite your story. I stand here as proof that even after years of pain and darkness you can create a life filled with love, success, and purpose.

Destiny isn't something you wait for, and it's certainly not something you simply accept and bear. It is something you *claim*.

Every step forward, no matter how small, is a declaration that you refuse to be defined by your past. You were born to do more than just survive—you were born to live, to thrive, and to shine.

About Nancy

Nancy Wolff is a dynamic entrepreneur, an educator, and a Medicare specialist whose career spans over three decades. Her journey began in 1985 with the launch of a successful business, earning recognition for leadership, top sales, and community dedication—culminating in the Volunteer of the Year award from the Orange County (New York) Chamber of Commerce in 2014.

In the insurance industry for over two decades, she's a trusted Medicare adviser, guiding clients in seven states through the intricate maze, constant changes in the laws and evolving landscape. Nancy's commitment to integrity, honesty, empathy, compassion, and resilience demonstrates her advocacy for clear, reliable information to make critical decisions when finding affordable health care. She empowers individuals with this knowledge, ensuring confidence and support in their choices.

Nancy's passion for education extends far beyond insurance. As a lifelong learner and mentor, she has built and sustained multiple businesses with the guidance from experts, demonstrating the power of adaptability and perseverance. She understands that success comes from continual growth, a positive mindset, and learning from the wisdom of past generations.

Nancy's constant improvement is evident as she travels across the US for professional development and actively shares insights with business owners and ambitious entrepreneurs. She believes in the power of mentorship and networking, using her experiences to inspire others to take charge of their futures.

Her dedication to learning has allowed her to refine her skills while uplifting those around her. Whether through workshops, speaking engagements, or one-on-one mentorship, she is passionate about guiding others toward dreaming bigger.

Her AI certifications and expertise allow her to bridge the gap between traditional business practices and modern technological advancements, helping entrepreneurs integrate AI tools to innovate while improving efficiency, saving time, and doubling productivity.

Beyond her professional accomplishments, as a dedicated speaker, Nancy shares personal stories and valuable lessons about safeguarding personal and financial information. Having faced fraud and identity theft, she transformed challenges into opportunities for education. Her authenticity and commitment make her a trusted figure in her field.

Nancy was acknowledged with the Culture Keeper Award by her Master Networks Community for her personal achievements, her commitment to fostering strong relationships, and contributing to her community. Her inspiring journey—from launching businesses to overcoming challenging obstacles—serves as a powerful testament to determination, perseverance, resilience, and reinvention.

Nancy invites you to learn and grow with her. Connect via LinkedIn, at MeetNancy.com, or by calling 845-609-0629.

CHAPTER 13

BROKEN TO BOLD

Lessons from a Life Rebuilt

By Nat Trodahl

The noise of our bickering voices silenced when the banging started. It wasn't a normal knock. It was the kind of knock that lets you know that trouble is on the other side of the door.

Bang.

Bang.

Bang.

We all exchanged fearful looks as my mother opened the door to find a giant, intimidating man waving papers in his left hand and a gun in his right.

"Ma'am, you've got five minutes to get your things and get out." We were getting evicted.

Again.

I was in high school at the time, and evictions had become commonplace since my father abandoned us, leaving my mom with two young children and a third one on the way. My mother was Argentinian and had no skills, had no education, and barely spoke English. We grabbed what we could, shoved it into seven big, black trash bags, and waited at the curb for one of our few friends to pick us up.

I'll never forget the looks of disgust and judgment sent our way as people drove by us, forming their assumptions and then likely forgetting about us a minute later as they returned to their warm homes.

As an undocumented, homeless resident of Las Vegas, my childhood would be riddled with instability, volatility, and poverty. I didn't know it then, but by the time I would turn nineteen, my family would be uprooted forty-one times.

That particular night, we ended up living in a shed in someone's backyard clear across town in a rough neighborhood that showed little mercy to a poor immigrant family. I was terrified of being bullied or beat up, but more than that I was terrified that the low-income school I would now be attending would not provide the education I wanted to get.

And I needed that education—it was my only way out.

Fast-forward to today, and I am a speaker, a resilience strategist, and a business consultant helping professionals combat emotional reactivity and make leadership decisions that drive profit and growth.

But before I could lead anyone else, I had to learn to lead myself. I had to confront my fears, navigate uncertainty, and make deliberate choices that set me on a path forward. Today, my life is drastically different from the life I used to live, searching for food, using magazines as toilet paper, and praying that no one knocked on the door.

Yet it's those memories of the past that became the fuel for my future.

Through trial and error, I developed a system that became my guide: evaluate, de-escalate, and navigate. These three steps weren't just survival tools; they became the foundation of a leadership framework I would use to help others.

This system was born out of necessity, was refined through experience, and is now the cornerstone of how I teach others to lead themselves with purpose, power, and resilience.

It starts with evaluating your emotions, then de-escalating them, and finally, navigating the choppy waters of your programming so you can chart your path to a bright and beautiful future.

EVALUATE

The streets were dark as I walked, and I knew that danger could be lurking around any corner. I carried an uncapped pen, foolishly convinced I could use it as a weapon if anyone tried to grab me.

I was just fifteen years old and had decided I was not going to change schools. I was not going to be like my mother, moving place to place, ripping food stamps out of a booklet, with no idea where the next meal, roof, or dollar was going to come from.

No.

I would get out and live differently. So day after day I took this walk, setting my alarm for 4 a.m. and walking one mile to the nearest bus stop, where I would then ride for two hours clear across town to school.

Men would sometimes pull their cars up next to me, asking if I wanted a ride, and my heart would race as I prayed they'd drive away. The risk was worth it if it meant a different life, but nothing came easily. I tried to get a part-time job, but because I was undocumented, I was denied employment, which awakened a whole new collection of fears. Would I be deported? Would I even be able to go to college? There were days the struggle made me more determined than ever and days I could feel nothing but the pain of hope slipping away. It was around this time that my high school counselor, Mr. Wickliffe, noticed something was wrong and stepped in to make sure I had everything I needed. He gave me bus tokens to ride the bus. To him he was handing me a bag of coins, but to me it was a key to my freedom. He changed my life and probably saved it.

What I know now is that your history doesn't have to become your future. All that fear and humiliation I lived through was vital information. I was learning by contrast what I did and didn't like, what I would and would not tolerate.

I was shaping my own identity and little by little becoming the person I wanted to be.

The first step to emotional resilience is to pause for a moment to evaluate and observe your reactions to any situation at hand. This awareness allows you to identify triggers, creating a foundation for intentional and informed action.

But resilience doesn't stop there. I learned that not only does clarity come from contrast—from getting crystal clear on what you *don't* want—but you need a goal that is so compelling it pulls you forward even when the odds are stacked against you.

You must also be willing to do what others won't so you can rise in ways they can't. It might sound crazy to get up in the middle of the night and ride for two hours to school, but to me it was a necessary step to liberation.

Every 4 a.m. alarm, every dangerous walk, and every moment of uncertainty was a step in claiming the life I wanted.

When we take time to evaluate our emotions, we are making a conscious decision to keep moving forward, no matter what, with the knowledge that every small act of courage brings you closer to the life you were meant to lead.

Years later I found Mr. Wickliffe and reached out to tell him that he was my hero.

"No, Nat," he said. "You are mine."

DE-ESCALATE

One of the tricky things our past will do is creep up on us when we least expect it and when it makes the least amount of sense.

In 2017 I had everything I wanted. I was happily married, making great money, and living in a beautiful home.

So there was no logic to the pain I felt, no logic to the desire I had to punch a hole through the wall. No rhyme or reason to the debate I was having with myself about whether I could scream without my husband hearing.

I had endured so much humiliation as a child, yet none of it compared with how I was feeling that morning. My mother and I still had a volatile relationship. My brothers, whom I had practically raised, wanted nothing to do with me, and I was overweight, in debt, and wondering how, after all the work I had done, I had landed back in this dark place.

I was the unhappiest I'd ever been, and for the first time, I looked at my leg and considered cutting it, rationalizing that maybe the pain of the blade would dull the pain in my heart. Luckily, I heard a voice in my head telling me to get up.

It was right around this time that a stranger handed me a book that would change my life. It was called *Connecting Paradigms: A Trauma-Informed and Neurobiological Framework for Motivational Interviewing Implementation*. I learned for the first time that what was happening to me was due to the adversity and neglect I'd lived through. I wasn't crazy. My past had had *biological* effects. My brain had literally retrained itself to look for trauma! This was a stunning realization that led to me reading a series of other books, which eventually led me to visiting the Zen Center of Las Vegas. There I learned to meditate and chant mantras, which helped to regulate my nervous system and rewire my brain for success, faith, and gratitude.

That's when it hit me. I had learned to evaluate my emotions but had not yet learned to de-escalate them. Once you've evaluated, the next step is to regain control with self-regulation techniques that help you shift from a reactive state to a reflective mindset.

You can learn to sit with what's happening, evaluate the triggered emotions it brings, and manage your reaction before it derails you into a downward spiral.

Over time I reconnected with my brothers and shifted how I interacted with them. I let go of my tendency to be the authority and allowed myself to just be their sister, accepting them for who they were and expressing love rather than disdain. We became closer than ever, and I am an aunt to their children. It took time, but I learned how to partner with my brain to change how I processed situations, which in turn shifted how I responded to them.

What I've learned is this: Triggers from the past don't announce themselves. They feel real and often mask themselves as logical reactions to the present. But here's how to spot the difference:

1. **Pause and ask questions.** When you're overwhelmed by emotion, pause and ask yourself, "What am I really reacting to?" Is this about what's happening right now, or does it feel familiar, like something from the past?

2. **Notice the intensity.** If your reaction feels disproportionate to the situation—more intense or emotional than the moment warrants—it's likely a trigger. Triggers often bring feelings such as fear, shame, or anger that seem larger than life.

3. **Ground yourself in the present.** When you suspect a trigger, use grounding techniques to bring yourself back to the present. Breathe deeply and focus on your physical surroundings.

Once you've identified a trigger, the next step is to de-escalate. Practice deep, rhythmic breathing to calm your nervous system. Name the emotion to reduce its power. Simply saying, "I feel angry," or, "I feel scared," helps your brain process the emotion more rationally. Use affirmations such as, "This moment is temporary, and I am safe," to shift your focus and regulate your emotions. Remind yourself of your current reality to draw a line between past and present. By learning to evaluate and de-escalate my emotions, I rebuilt relationships, restructured my inner world, and changed the trajectory of my life. I went from feeling trapped by my past to feeling liberated by the tools I'd gained.

Today, I share these lessons with others so they can take control of their own lives. You don't have to be at the mercy of your triggers. With practice, you can learn to spot them, defuse them, and respond to life with clarity and confidence.

When you take charge of your emotional reactions, you take charge of your life.

NAVIGATE

Teaching at the college level was never part of my plan, but when my brother needed financial help, I took a part-time job teaching at the University of Nevada, Las Vegas.

I was terrible, and the student reviews were humiliating. What I didn't realize at the time was that this failure was setting the stage for my growth.

Years later I was hired for a role requiring me to present to a room of sixty-plus community professionals. The fear was over-whelming, but I evaluated where this fear was coming from (the past teaching gig), and I de-escalated my emotions and stayed grounded in the present moment. I realized that my time at UNLV had taught me that discomfort and failure are often the best training grounds for growth. I leaned in to the fear, stepped into the role, and discovered my ability to connect, engage, and inspire through speaking.

We often don't realize we are navigating our own destiny while we're in the middle of it, but that experience set me on the path I'm on today. What started as a failure became the foundation of my work as a professional speaker and consultant. Now I teach others how to manage their emotions, navigate fear, and trans-form setbacks into stepping stones. This shift didn't just change my career—it reshaped how I view obstacles, turning them into opportunities for resilience, growth, and impact.

Embrace discomfort as a natural part of transformation, knowing that every stumble is an opportunity to rise stronger.

When you can train yourself to do this, obstacles transform into opportunities and fear becomes a catalyst for success. Remember, your past may have influenced you, but it's the choices you make now that define your future.

Shaping Your Own Dream

The most life-changing truth I've learned through every challenge, every setback, and every unexpected twist is this: No one is coming to shape your dream for you. The life you want—the freedom, the success, the fulfillment—is carved from the raw material of your circumstances.

My mother sacrificed everything trying to achieve the American dream, and it made me determined to define what that meant for me. Shaping your dream starts with evaluating the truth of your situation without excuses or blame. Only then can you take the reins and decide what comes next.

It continues with the courage to de-escalate, to silence the noise of fear and doubt, and steady yourself in the storm.

Finally, shaping your dream is about navigating forward, one deliberate step at a time. I learned to embrace the willingness to do what most others won't. Whether it meant studying late into the night, working through exhaustion, or choosing persistence when quitting seemed easier, I committed to taking those extra steps others might shy away from. That willingness to keep moving even when the path was hard has been critical to the realization of my destiny.

I now have a loving family, a career I love, and the ability to write donation checks to the same organizations that helped my family and me in the height of our struggles. It is a dream come true.

Your dreams are waiting for you too, and the time to act is now—not when circumstances are perfect or when fear finally leaves you.

No one is coming to save you, and that's the most liberating truth of all because it means the power to shape your life, to claim your dreams, and to rewire your brain for joy and success has always been, and will *always* be, right in your own hands.

About Nat

Nat Trodahl knows what it takes to overcome challenges. She grew up with an immigrant parent, facing extreme poverty, constant instability, and even homelessness. But she refused to let her circumstances define her. Instead, she turned struggle into strength, using resilience and emotional intelligence to build a life and career focused on helping others do the same.

Now, with over fifteen years of experience, Nat helps business leaders and teams think clearly and act decisively under stress, handle tough situations, and create stronger, more successful workplaces. Her approach blends personal storytelling with practical strategies, teaching people how to manage emotions, solve problems, and lead with confidence—even in high-stakes moments.

Nat's message is clear: When you learn to manage yourself first, you can handle anything life throws your way.

When she's not speaking or coaching, Nat loves baking, hiking, tap dancing, and spending time with her husband, Sean, and their son, Sullivan, in Boulder City, Nevada.

To connect with Nat, visit nattrodahl.com or call 702-763-2448.

CHAPTER 14

UNSTOPPABLE

The Art of Rising Again

By Gwen Medved

I used to think resilience was about gritting my teeth and pushing through. That success was about mastering the art of holding it all together. That abundance was reserved for those who had a straight-line path to victory, not for those of us who had been cracked open by life's storms.

I was wrong.

Resilience isn't about never breaking. It's about learning how to rebuild. It's about seeing every detour, every heartbreak, every gut-wrenching loss as a sacred invitation to rise higher, stronger, more aligned with who we are meant to be.

And success? It's not about chasing. It's about *allowing*. It is about trusting that every challenge is carving a deeper space within us to receive more—more wisdom, more love, more abundance, more *us*.

I know this now because life has given me the lessons—wrapped in disappointment, betrayal, and loss. And it has been my job, my *privilege*, to unwrap them, hold them up to the light, and decide: Will this break me? Or will it build me?

LESSON 1: THE BREAKING IS THE BECOMING

The day I realized my life wasn't going as planned, I was standing in the wreckage of everything I thought was certain. The marriage I had bet my life on had dissolved into a truth I didn't want to face. The financial security I had worked tirelessly for was slipping through my fingers. The vision I had for my future felt as if it belonged to someone else—someone who no longer existed.

I wanted to fix it. Patch it up. Put on the "I'm fine" mask and keep going. But something inside me whispered, "This is your moment. Let it break you. Let it shape you into who you are becoming."

So I surrendered. I let go of the version of me that was clinging to what was. And in the stillness of that surrender, I felt it—*the seed of something new*. The whisper of a purpose I had been too busy surviving to hear.

What in your life is asking to be released? What are you holding on to that no longer fits the person you are becoming? What if instead of resisting the breaking, you trusted that it was leading you to something greater? Here's the truth: The things that break us? They aren't punishments. They're assignments. They are here to crack us open so the truest, boldest, most unstoppable version of us can emerge.

LESSON 2: SUCCESS IS A DECISION, NOT A DESTINATION

I used to believe that success was a place I would arrive at one day—a mountaintop, a finish line, a golden moment where everything finally made sense. But what I've learned is this: Success isn't a destination. It's a decision we make over and over again, even when—especially when—it feels impossible.

Success is deciding to get back up when you've been knocked down so many times that the ground feels like home. Success is choosing to believe in your dream when no one else can see it yet. Success is standing in the middle of your storm and declaring, "This will not define me. I will use this. I will alchemize this into something beautiful."

The most successful people aren't the ones who never fall. They're the ones who refuse to stay down. Where in your life are you waiting for permission to succeed? What if success wasn't something you had to chase but something you could claim right now? What would shift if you decided—today—that you are already worthy?

LESSON 3: ABUNDANCE FLOWS TO THOSE WHO TRUST

For most of my life, I believed abundance had to be earned. That I had to prove I was worthy of love, success, and financial security. That I had to work harder, sacrifice more, be *better* in order to deserve a life of ease and joy.

And then life, in its infinite wisdom, took away everything I thought I had control over. My plans unraveled. My safety nets disappeared. And I was left with only one choice: to trust. To trust that when one door closes, it's because something greater is waiting. To trust that I am inherently worthy—not because of what I achieve but because of who I am. To trust that the universe isn't conspiring against me—it's conspiring *for* me.

Where in your life are you gripping too tightly, trying to control the outcome? What would happen if you loosened your grip and allowed abundance to flow? How would your life change if you truly believed you are already enough?

The moment I let go of the belief that I had to force and fight for abundance, I felt it start to flow toward me. Opportunities I never saw coming. Connections that felt divinely orchestrated. Financial blessings that arrived in ways I couldn't have planned if I tried. Abundance isn't a prize for the perfect. It's a natural by-product of alignment, trust, and faith.

LESSON 4: THE GIFT IS IN THE OBSTACLE

I know it doesn't feel like it when you're in the thick of it, when life is rearranging itself in ways that feel unfair, unbearable, and utterly confusing, but *every single obstacle you face is here to elevate you.*

Your heartbreak? It's teaching you what you truly deserve. Your failure? It's redirecting you toward something even greater. Your betrayal? It's refining your circle, showing you who's truly meant to walk this journey with you. What obstacle are you facing right now that feels insurmountable? What if instead of resisting it, you leaned in and asked, "What is this here to teach me?" How could this moment be preparing you for something greater?

Nothing is random. Nothing is wasted. Everything— *everything*—is guiding you home to yourself.

LESSON 5: YOU ARE UNSTOPPABLE WHEN YOU CHOOSE TO BE

If you take nothing else from this chapter, take this: *You are unstoppable the moment you decide to be.* The moment you decide that nothing—no failure, no heartbreak, no setback—will define you. The moment you decide to see the lesson instead of the loss. The moment you decide that you are worthy of everything you desire, simply because you exist.

Life will test you. It will push you. It will ask you, again and again, "Are you ready to rise?" And I hope with everything in me that your answer will always be yes.

My love, you were born to rise. You were born to break barriers. You were born to turn obstacles into stepping stones, pain into purpose, and setbacks into comebacks. You were born to be *unstoppable.*

UNSTOPPABLE: WRITING A NEW SCRIPT

I spent thirty years building a life. A marriage. A home. A family.

For three decades I poured myself into a story I believed in, a script I followed to the letter—the one that said if you work hard enough, love fiercely enough, sacrifice enough, you'll get the happily ever after, that white picket fence of certainty. And then, one day, that life crumbled.

The marriage that was supposed to last forever ended. The family structure I had nurtured shattered. The future I had planned no longer existed. I stood at the edge of what felt like ruin and had to ask myself a terrifying question: Who am I now?

I could have let fear write the next chapter. I could have let the loss consume me, let the grief anchor me to a past that no longer wanted me. But instead, I made a different choice. I chose *love*. Not the love that tries to hold on to something that's already gone. Not the love that begs to be chosen by someone who has already turned away. I chose self-love. Radical, unshakable, world-altering self-love. I chose to believe that my story wasn't over—it was just beginning.

FEAR DESTROYS; LOVE CREATES

If there's one thing I've learned through this, it's this: Love is the creator of abundance. Fear is the destroyer of it.

Fear contracts. It tightens its grip, clings to what no longer serves us, suffocates possibilities before they have the chance to bloom.

Fear tells us, "You'll never rebuild. You're too broken. You're too old. You're too much or not enough." And if we listen to fear long enough, we start to believe it. We stay small. We live inside the ruins instead of stepping forward to build something new.

But love—love expands. Love opens. Love *trusts* that even in the unraveling, something greater is being woven together. Love tells us, "You are more than this moment of pain. There is abundance waiting for you on the other side of this loss. You are not starting over. You are rising higher."

Choosing love over fear isn't just a mindset shift. It's an *actionable resilience strategy*. It's the difference between staying stuck and stepping into the life you were meant to live. Here's what that looked like for me.

RESILIENCE IN ACTION

I had every reason to let fear define me. To let my broken marriage be the story people knew me by. To let the grief of losing the family unit I built keep me paralyzed. To let the uncertainty of my future drown me in doubt. But I refused.

Instead, I picked up the pen and started writing a new script.

1. I let go to make space for more.

I stopped clinging to what was. I grieved—deeply, fully, with my whole body—but I didn't let the grief become my identity. I chose to believe that the love I had given, the lessons I had learned, and even the pain I had endured had a purpose. Letting go didn't mean erasing the past. It meant making room for a bigger, bolder, more aligned future. And now I ask you, What are you still holding on to that no longer serves you? Is it a relationship that has run its course? A version of yourself that no longer fits? A dream that was built for a past version of you?

Letting go is not an act of defeat—it is an act of faith. It is trusting that what is ahead is far greater than anything behind you. Your next chapter cannot begin if your hands are still gripping the last one. So loosen your grip. Breathe. Make space. The life that is meant for you needs room to arrive.

2. I built my own abundance.

For years I had tied my security to a shared life. But when that life ended, I had a choice: shrink in fear or step into my own power. I chose abundance. I invested in myself. My dreams. My financial future. My healing. I decided that I am my own source of security. Not a marriage. Not a bank account. Me.

And from that place of confidence, abundance started flowing, because when you operate from a belief in your own worthiness, the universe responds. Where are you giving your power away?

Are you waiting for someone else to make you feel safe? Are you telling yourself that you'll be abundant when the circumstances are just right?

You don't have to wait. You *are* the source. You are capable of creating more than you've ever imagined, but first, you must believe it. Start claiming the life that is already waiting for you.

3. I made joy my compass.

Fear tells you to stay safe. To avoid risks. To protect yourself from future pain. Love tells you to *live*. So I did. I traveled. I surrounded myself with women who lifted me higher. I threw myself into my work, my mission, my calling. I laughed—real, belly-deep laughter I hadn't felt in years. I refused to let the end of my marriage be the end of my happiness. When was the last time you truly felt joy—not just contentment, not just *getting through the day*, but real, unfiltered, full-bodied joy?

Maybe it's time to stop waiting for joy to find you and start chasing it instead. Life is meant to be *lived*, not just endured. Take the trip. Say yes to new experiences. Let yourself be surrounded by people who remind you how beautiful life can be.

EVERYTHING IS A LESSON; EVERY LESSON IS A GIFT

This experience—this breaking apart of everything I knew—could have made me bitter. It could have made me afraid of love, of abundance, of risk.

Instead, it freed me. It gave me the greatest lesson of all: Nothing is happening *to* me. Everything is happening *for* me. Every ending is an invitation to a new beginning. Every loss is a clearing for something greater. Every obstacle is a gift—if we are brave enough to receive it. And I am unstoppable because I choose to see it that way.

So if you are standing at the edge of your own breaking, wondering if you will ever feel whole again, hear me when I say this: You will. You will rise. You will rebuild. You will love again— deeper, wilder, more freely than ever before. You will laugh in ways you never imagined. You will wake up one day and realize you are not just surviving. You are *thriving*.

The person you are becoming? They are unstoppable.

About Gwen

Gwen Medved is a best-selling author, an entrepreneur, and an advocate for women and children, known for her deep commitment to family and impactful storytelling. Gwen works with individuals and companies dedicated to making a positive difference and is on a mission to inspire others to see the opportunities hidden inside every obstacle.

Gwen has been featured in *Forbes*, *USA Today*, *Women's Health*, and *Entrepreneur* magazine, and has appeared on ABC, NBC, CBS, and FOX affiliates nationwide, as well as Yahoo! News, CNBC, and MSNBC.

A member of The National Academy of Best-Selling Authors, Gwen is a recipient of both the EXPY and Quilly awards. She is the executive producer of the Telly Award-winning film *It's Happening Right Here*, which raises awareness about child sex trafficking in the US.

Gwen holds a BA from Purdue University and an MEd in counseling and human services from DePaul University. She is a certified Canfield Transformational Trainer, Values-Based Leadership Coach, Health Coach, and a dedicated advocate for women, children, and families.

In her personal life, Gwen enjoys traveling and spending time with family and friends in the Midwest and Santa Monica, California. Her goals include lake house living with backyard chickens.

CHAPTER 15

IGNITE

Breaking Free and Burning Bright

By Sara Wolfe

The glass of wine trembled in my hand as I lowered myself to the floor, tears rolling down my face.

The weight of nearly three decades in a deeply dysfunctional relationship pressed down on me, each memory flickering like a scene in a film. The instability—the financial devastation, the emotional turmoil, the moments I questioned my worth—had carved deep marks on my soul. After yet another moment that shook me to my core, I knew something had to change. My dog rested his head on my lap, his silent trust a stark contrast to the chaos I felt inside. I stared into the glass of wine and suddenly saw the hollow reflection of someone I didn't recognize.

Who was this woman? How had I become her? The realization hit me like a thunderclap: I had lost myself completely, and it was time to take control—to reshape the shattered fragments of my identity into someone I could finally be proud of.

To come home to myself.

I had grown up living all over the world, in a religious household where divorce was considered taboo. While this instilled in me values of perseverance and commitment, it also delayed my understanding of knowing when to let go of what no longer serves us.

As a young girl, I was forbidden to show my legs or wear makeup. I desperately wanted to fit in, but the restrictions I lived under, combined with frequent moves and an emotionally distant home life, left me feeling isolated and unseen. I would later come to understand some of the challenges my father was facing at the time, but as a child, all I felt was absence.

"Be quiet. Be invisible."

"Stay humble and obedient, and never ever assert yourself."

"You wouldn't want to appear bossy or proud."

Those were the messages drilled into me as a child, so it's no wonder that at just seventeen years old I found myself in a relationship with a man who expected submissiveness. The early signs of dysfunction were clear, but I adhered to the values instilled in me as a child and stayed.

And stayed.

And stayed.

For nearly three decades, my four children and I endured profound instability—homelessness, utilities being shut off without warning, and the constant fear of displacement. But the deepest wound wasn't the physical hardship—it was the crushing weight of pretending everything was OK. Behind closed doors we lived a reality few could imagine, while outwardly trying to keep up appearances.

You see, my family was very active in our church. My husband was a church elder, and together we held leadership roles that placed us in prominent positions in the church. We had invested heavily in real estate, and when the market crashed in 2008, we lost everything, tipping our already fractured life into total chaos. We lost our beautiful home, our cars, and our sense of identity. The irony kept me awake at night—on the outside we were the picture-perfect church family. But behind closed doors I felt as if I was unraveling. I wore the mask of the ideal wife while privately enduring shame and confusion. My children too were caught in the emotional storm, struggling under the weight of a life that didn't match what others saw.

And no one suspected a thing.

We moved between sixteen different homes in the years that followed, piecing life back together only to watch it fall apart again and again, my husband finding but never keeping odd jobs and my children growing painfully aware of our reality. Over the years, I had embarked on a deep journey of personal discovery, reading books, creating practices for self-regulation, and forming communities of women around me. But while those seeds of resilience were being planted, it would take years of deprograming for them to finally break through.

The day I ended up on the hallway floor with a wine glass had been particularly painful. I was in line at the grocery store, paying for our groceries with our government-issued SNAP card, and the cashier had trouble with the payment. The people in line were growing restless, and I could feel their judging eyes. She called the manager over for help, loudly announcing that she was having trouble with my food stamps. But that wasn't the worst part. The devastating blow came when she tilted her head and said, "You're Camille's mom, aren't you?"

My heart sank. Do I deny my daughter to save her the humiliation or admit it, exposing her to judgment and ridicule by her peers? That moment sent me into despair. It was also the moment that ignited a fire inside me. I would not stay on that floor. I would not continue to let life happen to me. I would unleash and embody the identity of the woman I knew I could be. I would stand up and become a cocreator with God.

I would love to say that I left that day, but I didn't. Five long years later, armed with tools from therapy, a stubborn resolve, and a fierce commitment to reconstruct my identity, I finally filed for divorce.

Ignite Your Life

The road to reclamation is not a short or linear one. It winds and climbs and dips. It's smooth one day and riddled with obstacles the next. But if we can stay on that road, eyes fixed on a spot in the future, something happens to us.

On that road we become who we are meant to be.

I didn't *see* it happening, but during those years of struggle and heartache my soul was being fortified, shaped, and molded into who I now know is my most purposeful self.

My story is one of navigating immense challenges, rediscovering my worth, and rebuilding my life from the ground up, yet it isn't all that unique. Each of us has endured some form of shame. Every one of us has, at some point, made ourselves smaller, contracted under the weight of other people's opinions and expectations. Each of us has found ourselves on some version of the dark hallway floor, wondering how we got there and determined to get back up.

There's a saying that whatever awakens us isn't nearly as important as what it awakens in us. The catalyst for change pales in importance to the change itself. It doesn't matter what prompts us to take control of our lives; it only matters that we do.

Today, I'm blessed to work with clients all over the world, helping them unlock their limitless potential. I host masterminds, offer VIP coaching, and help entrepreneurs launch health-and-wellness businesses.

After years of research, I developed the IGNITE Framework to help people break through limitations and step into their highest potential. It is a powerful system that acts as a road map to the reclamation of one's *identity*. By igniting change in your life, you embark on a powerful journey that helps you leverage the challenges you've faced, alchemizing dark into light, pain into progress, and confusion into a stunning clarity that reveals to you exactly who you were born to be!

Identify Your Truths

The first step to igniting change is to identify the beliefs and patterns keeping you stuck.

Most of us hold beliefs that were handed down by parents, teachers, or religion when we were too young to question them.

These borrowed truths may have served someone else's values

but now conflict with the ones we've developed as adults. Like a mark on our body we no longer notice, these beliefs run silently in the background, scripting our actions and shaping our reality without our awareness. It's time to bring them to light, question their validity, and replace them with truths that align with who you are *today*!

What have you accepted as truths? What long-held beliefs no longer resonate? Becoming who we're meant to be requires the courage to let go of the version of us that was crafted by others. It's uncomfortable. When you step closer to your core identity, it will feel like being asked to remove a comfortable sweater you've worn for years. People won't recognize you without that sweater. They may even resent you for taking it off. Once you do, however, you'll realize how restricting it had been. You'll move differently. Boldly.

Free.

GROUND YOURSELF FOR GROWTH

One of the most common traps we fall into is being carried along a current. Ask a kid what they want to be when they grow up, and they'll excitedly tell you the vision they have for their much-anticipated adult life.

By the time adulthood arrives, they've forgotten all about those dreams and are instead following a flow of life that has been dictated by others. One of the keys to reclaiming your identity is to reestablish connection with yourself and the vision you have for your best life.

What do you want? How much money do you want to make? Who is your ideal partner? How do you spend your day?

When you start crafting a vision for the life you want, you may realize how much your current life is in direct opposition to it.

That's your permission slip to change.

Navigate with Alignment as Your Compass

The look on my son's face haunts me to this day.

After years of emotional strain and escalating tension in our home, I made the excruciating decision to enroll him in a therapeutic program for teens in crisis. The environment he had grown up in had taken a toll on all of us. I was witnessing him lose control in ways that scared me—and broke my heart. When the day came, I let him go, believing it was the most loving choice I could make at the time, even if it shattered me.

After enduring nearly three decades of dysfunction, peace is a core value for me, and my son's behavior had made peace impossible. Choosing alignment isn't always easy. Sometimes it requires us to make the hardest decisions of our lives—to set boundaries and change the parts of our lives that no longer serve us. These are painful sacrifices, but we've got to trust that our inner compass will always lead us where we need to go.

Today, my son is thriving. The program gave him the space to form his own identity outside the storm of our household. It wasn't just a turning point for him—it was one for me too. When I work with clients, this step is often the hardest: making those tough decisions that honor your values and vision. It requires faith, connection to a higher power, and deep self-awareness. Take a moment to reflect: What are your values? Who do you see yourself as? What in your life no longer aligns with that vision? Where do you need to set boundaries to create space for peace and purpose? The answers to these questions hold the key to your alignment—and your freedom.

Integrate Science and Spirit

Integrating spirit with science is one of the keys to reclaiming your life because it bridges the gap between practical, evidence-based strategies and the deeper, soulful alignment that drives lasting transformation.

With my clients and in my own life, I integrate tools such as cognitive behavioral techniques (CBT), neuroplasticity, and NLP anchoring to reframe limiting beliefs and shift subconscious patterns.

Cutting-edge techniques that enhance emotional resilience and gratitude practices—proven to boost dopamine and serotonin—cultivate intention-based transformation. This holistic integration creates the sustainable transformation necessary to reclaim the life you deserve.

Make time for rituals and practices that restore your energy and foster clarity. It's in these practices that you learn the language of your own heart.

Transform Into the Hero of Your Own Story

Every great story begins with a stirring—a call from within whispering of something greater. You feel it, don't you—that pull, telling you that you're meant for more?

This is the start of your hero's journey, a path that challenges you to step into your power, break through limits, and embody the highest version of yourself. But here's the truth: It won't be easy. There will be dragons to slay, dark nights of the soul to endure, and moments that test your faith. These challenges aren't obstacles; they're the very fire that forges you.

I remember the moment I felt my own call to adventure. I was preparing for a keynote speech, unsure if my story was worth sharing, when I stumbled upon Lisa Nichols. Her words moved me to tears and reminded me of who I was meant to be. In that moment, I knew I was a storyteller. That realization wasn't just about speaking on a stage; it was about stepping fully into my purpose and owning my power. What is the whisper in your soul calling you toward? Have you ignored it or convinced yourself it wasn't meant for you?

The journey to becoming the hero of your own story requires courage. It asks you to leave behind the familiar and face the unknown. It's uncomfortable, but within the discomfort lies transformation. Think about the struggles you've faced. What if they weren't signs that you were off track but markers of growth, proof that you're being shaped for something greater?

Expand Your Impact

One of the most important lessons I've learned over time is that our struggles are not our shame—they are our strength. Every scar you've endured has the power to light someone else's path.

When we stop hiding what we've been through and start owning it, we unlock a ripple effect of impact that reaches far beyond what we can imagine. By sharing your experiences, you don't just heal yourself; you inspire others to believe in what's possible for their own lives.

If you knew that your story was the key to someone else's breakthrough, would you be brave enough to tell it?

Choose Who You Are

Wolfe is not my maiden name. It is my chosen name.

When it was time to reclaim my identity and start living my purpose, I took myself through a visioning exercise, decided the qualities I wanted to embody and express, and chose a name that aligned with those qualities.

In many cultures the wolf is a sacred creature that symbolizes strength and an unwavering perseverance that allows it to survive against all odds.

A wolf leads by its intuition and even in the dark forest knows its way.

Just like wolves, I am very independent, but I also believe that the strength of the pack is in the wolf and the strength of the wolf is in the pack. Together we can accomplish great things.

Each of us is free to choose who we are and the ways we use our challenges to make an impact in the world.

For me every heartbreak and every moment spent on that cold hallway floor were shaping me for the work I do today. Those trials weren't meant to break me; they were meant to prepare me. The dragons I've faced have all been necessary to reveal my strength and ignite the fire inside me.

Your journey, like mine, is an ever-evolving masterpiece, with each chapter leading you closer to who you're meant to be. You are not defined by the moments that brought you to your knees.

You are defined by how you *rise*.

About Sara

Sara Wolfe doesn't just teach transformation—she *embodies* it. From childhood trauma and nearly three decades in a relationship that drained her spirit and fractured her sense of self, to losing everything and rebuilding from scratch, she's proof that rock bottom isn't the end; it's the launchpad.

Now she's a global force in business strategy, high-performance leadership, and personal reinvention, working with entrepreneurs across six continents who refuse to play small.

Through her IGNITE Framework, she's helped visionaries break through fear, redefine success, and create businesses that don't just make money but make impact.

She's not here for surface-level success. If you're looking for another hustle-until-you-collapse guru, keep scrolling. Sara's about smart, sustainable growth, wealth without burnout, and power without pretense. She helps high achievers stop spinning their wheels and start stepping into their true influence—on stages, in boardrooms, and in life.

Her work isn't just about making shifts; it's about starting a movement, a revolution of bold thinkers, disrupters, and trailblazers who are done waiting for permission and ready to build empires on their own terms.

Your past isn't an anchor. It's fuel. Now light the damn fire.

Learn more at SaraWolfe.global.

CHAPTER 16

AGAINST THE GRAIN

From Pain to Purpose

By Dr. Stacey Kevin Frick

was only three years old, but I'll never forget the feeling of the carpet pressing against my cheek as my father's massive body crushed me into the floor.

I couldn't move, couldn't breathe.

His weight was suffocating, and my seven-year-old sister, painfully aware of the cost of interfering, sat motionless in a chair.

He called it wrestling, but there was no playfulness in the way he grabbed me and pinned me down. My face smashed into the carpet, and each shallow breath brought less oxygen and less hope for getting away.

After what seemed like an eternity, my body went limp, and the world went black.

I eventually came to, and my sister later told me she'd been paralyzed until she heard me sobbing. Not even then did she dare to move and come for me.

This was my father's nature, a man who tied shoelaces to the tails of cats and threw them over clotheslines, who caught bees and let them sting his brother's arms for fun. He was six feet, four inches and 230 pounds of anger, rage, and violence.

When I was fourteen, my mother found the courage to leave him under the protection of a man she'd met and would eventually marry. It didn't take long to realize that her new life would not be a safe space for me either. Her husband was past the stage of raising teenagers, and one day after an argument, I got on my bike and rode to a friend's house. When I called my mother to ask when I should come back, she replied, "I think it is best that you stay there."

She showed up with my belongings, handed my friend's mother twenty dollars, and said, "Thank you."

I stayed with that family for months, until my father found out and came to get me.

At fifteen, I went back to living with him and back to living in fear for my life. By the age of eighteen my tolerance for his abuse had reached its breaking point.

I decided that college was my way out, and I went to take the ACT exam. The problem was, he wanted something from me that day as well.

"Where were you?" he demanded.

"Taking college entrance exams," I said, my voice steady.

"I needed you," he snapped. "I had to unload this lawnmower by myself."

"You didn't tell me you needed my help," I replied defiantly. "And I'm going to college."

He didn't like that. It meant he'd lose control.

"I'll take your TV away," he said.

"I don't care," I shot back.

"I'll take your phone away."

"I don't care."

"What if I take your car away?" he said, his voice rising.

"I bought my car," I said, meeting his gaze. "So that would be stealing."

He stepped closer, his fist clenched. "You're about to get your face broken."

I stood up. "I'll be outside," I said, walking past him.

I waited, and for a moment, I was convinced he was looking for his gun to shoot me, but he never came out. I left without looking back.

From that moment on, I was on my own. I paid fifty dollars a month to sleep on someone's sofa and worked four jobs to make it through college, each step a hero's challenge toward reclaiming my life. It was hard.

But I was free. Almost.

Pathways for Success

My early life was riddled with violence. The city I lived in was known as the meth capital of the world, and fear ruled the streets. Violence was a normal part of life. Death was so normalized that schoolmates getting on my bus crying because their brother had been killed and his body had been left in a field along my bus route barely phased me.

I realized at a young age that I had an internal authenticity that didn't resonate with my environment. Every aspect of my surroundings felt wrong. That feeling motivated me to seek out my own path—one that resonated with my heart.

I didn't realize it then, but I was learning, by contrast, what resonated with me and what didn't. I was forging beliefs that would become the bedrock of a new identity and would eventually be tools I used to help others.

You see, when I left my father's house, I made up my mind that it would be a fresh start. The victimized kid was gone, and in his place was a grown man, with vision, courage, and an unwavering commitment to become everything my father wasn't.

Today, after practicing medicine for over twenty years and serving as CEO of multiple successful businesses, I've chosen to dedicate my life to empowering individuals to build lives of joy, abundance, and authenticity.

As the founder of a human potential development, I've merged my business acumen with holistic well-being practices to create transformative pathways for success.

These practices, for me, are the cornerstone of a life well lived, and if you try them, you'll likely find yourself redefining success, reclaiming lost bits of your identity, and eventually becoming exactly the person you were meant to be.

MEET YOURSELF IN THE SPACE BETWEEN

From the moment we're born, we are inundated with messages designed to shape our understanding of the world. These messages often steer us *toward* conformity and *away from* self-discovery. This creates a dissonance within us, fostering insecurity until we barely recognize ourselves in the costume we're wearing.

Years of abuse had instilled a belief in me that I was unlovable. I realize now that I became an overachiever in the hopes that if I did great things, I'd feel and be worthy of love.

At some point it occurred to me that the best way to prove my worth was to become a medical doctor.

One day in college my professor asked to see me after class. He told me that his wife was my genetics professor and that my physiology professor was his best friend. I struggled to figure out what that had to do with me when he suddenly said, "You applied for the medical honor society. I'm the chair. You're not going to get in."

I felt as if my dreams were being crushed on the spot, and seeing my crestfallen face, he continued talking.

"We've all noticed that when you don't like a subject, you're a C student at best. However, if there's a topic you're interested in, you're the best in class and no one is even close. Have you thought about something other than medicine?"

I hadn't, but it was clear I was being urged to. The truth is, I hadn't thought much about any of it. I put myself on a track I thought would act as evidence of my worth. He handed me an invitation to visit the veterinary college. When I went there, I experienced a feeling I'd never felt before. I realized I would do this work for free. If all I had was food, shelter, and this work, that would be enough. I let go of medical school, applied to veterinary college, and was finally on a path that aligned with my future purpose and not the narrative my history had written.

Or so I thought.

It turns out that while I was doing work I loved, I was still seeking something to fill the voids left by childhood. I discovered what Saint Aquinas described as the four idols: money, power, pleasure, and fame. I had my own practice, worked eighty hours or more a week, made a lot of money, and enjoyed the status of being the boss.

Eventually it took its toll.

I realized that money and power should never be goals. When they are goals, you can never have enough. What they should be are natural consequences of your service to others. I'd grown up in such emotional poverty that I ended up adopting society's opinion that people who were wealthy and powerful were worthy and valid. The voice of my heart had been drowned out by the fleeting highs that come with overachieving.

When this happens, we must pause. In the stillness we can begin to feel the subtle differences between the noise of external expectations and the solid, enduring presence of what truly matters to us.

Something clicked in me, and I started to analyze why I was the way I was. I began searching for my superpower and realized that at my core I was a gifted healer as a teacher. I was great at surgery and not so great at appointment work. I restructured my practice to align with my strengths, and that shift resulted in rapid business growth. Still, something was missing.

This is where the power of the pause can catapult you into the next chapter of your life.

When something feels out of sync, it's an invitation to be still. So often we feel that something is missing, so we try harder, which only moves us faster in the wrong direction.

Taking time to pause and reconnect to our values is paramount to gaining the clarity we need to choose our next direction.

Take a moment to think about your life. Are your actions aligned with your authenticity? Or are they echoes of the noise around you? Contrast this feeling with how you *want* to feel. What values rise to the surface when you silence the voices of others? What would you do if you had no fear of judgment? What would you *stop* doing if you were three times as brave?

This pause is where we begin to dismantle external influence and uncover the essence of who we are.

Once I had taken the time to pause and reflect, I realized my mission to serve with excellence would be compromised if my heart wasn't in the work. On paper I was a huge success.

But it was success in terms that no longer aligned with my values. So I sold everything. I gave it all up.

And I never felt happier or more successful.

SETTLE, DON'T SETTLE

One of the most transformative lessons I've learned is to settle without settling. It might sound as if those things are mutually exclusive, but they aren't. When we can learn to settle into the quiet power of our being, grounding ourselves in the truth of who we are but without settling for less than we want, we've struck that perfect balance between surrender and conviction.

We can move through life confident in our values and weigh our options against the benchmark of our own philosophies without the need for external validation.

Too often people tolerate circumstances that chip away at their essence, and they become depressed, having compromised their own principles. I encourage everyone to instead charge into change, adjusting their steps as many times as necessary until they've fallen into rhythm with life.

When I left medicine, I'd become the CEO of a multi-hospital system. When I felt I could no longer lead in a way that felt authentic, I left. I could have second-guessed that decision. After all, I'd achieved a level of success most people would call a dream come true. Yet I walked away from it without a single regret because I'd become fully attuned to who I was and would not live a life that contradicted that.

It didn't matter how shiny an opportunity was if taking it meant settling for less than full resonance. Conventional wisdom may have tricked you into believing that living this way would lead to less—less money, fewer accolades—and yet I've found the opposite to be true.

I now have a completed manuscript for my own book, I'm coauthoring this book and others, and I'm the CEO of a company that allows me to express my purpose in service to others.

By not settling for everyone else's definition of *success*, you might just settle into the life you were meant to live.

How would it feel to wake up to a life that was an exact match to your values, beliefs, and mission? What would such a life look like?

Hopefully you can picture it, and if you can, you're ready for the next step.

ONE SMALL TIPTOE

I've found over the years that many people tend to skew wisdom, twisting it until it morphs from good advice into a recipe for self-sabotage.

"Shoot for the stars!" they say.

"Dream big!"

And perhaps the most damaging: "Go big or go home!"

It might be framed in an encouraging tone, but for many the idea of going big is so overwhelming that we prefer to go home!

My advice?

Tiptoe one step forward. I've made a habit of giving myself MTO goals—minimum, target, and outrageous goals.

If I want to lose ten pounds, the minimum target I'll set is to stop eating cookies before bed. It's simple, and I can guarantee I'll succeed at that. My outrageous goal might be to run a marathon. I probably won't, but if I keep celebrating minimum targets such as not eating cookies before bed and going to the gym, I eventually will have achieved my goal without overwhelming my mind.

Start each moment by taking one small action in the direction you want to feel.

You may indeed achieve your outrageous goal, but even if you don't, you're better off than when you started. And that's what life is about, right—waking up every day and recommitting to becoming our best selves?

What Happens *to* You Reveals What's Meant to Happen *for* You

My father passed away in 2000. When I think about him now, I feel only gratitude in my heart. My mother lives in Florida, and we have a good relationship. That might surprise you, but I wouldn't be who I am without *all* the pieces of my past.

My history has informed my present in the most profound way. That's possible for you too if you can learn to see all that happens *to* you as clues to what's meant to happen *for* you.

Imagine waking up every day with a deep sense of confidence, purpose, and excitement about the future, knowing *you* are in control of shaping your destiny. This is the ultimate expression of personal freedom.

Along the way, doubts will surface and challenges will test your resolve. However, every step forward reclaims a piece of your true self. When I paused long enough to truly listen, I heard the quiet call of my authentic self.

Every struggle led me to the realization that freedom isn't found in accomplishments but in alignment. It's found in the courage to live a life true to your values, regardless of the noise around you.

The space between pain and purpose is where transformation begins. It's where we strip away the layers of who we were told to be so we can find out who we are. So pause.

Meet yourself in the quiet. Learn about yourself in the falls, and when you rise, you'll be rising as the person you were always meant to be.

About Dr. Frick

Dr. Stacey Kevin Frick is a seasoned leader and visionary dedicated to fostering health, well-being, and financial empowerment. After practicing medicine for over twenty years and serving as CEO of multiple successful businesses, Dr. Frick now dedicates his life to empowering others to lead lives of fulfilling service. His mission is to guide individuals toward lives filled with joy, abundance, and purpose, grounded in authenticity and personal empowerment.

As the founder of a human potential development, Dr. Frick merges his extensive leadership expertise and business acumen with holistic well-being practices to create transformative pathways for success. A highly sought-after life coach, author, speaker, and entrepreneur, he specializes in boosting self-confidence, enhancing emotional intelligence, and fostering personal growth. His passion for helping individuals overcome personal and professional barriers defines his career and legacy.

Dr. Frick's journey reflects a multifaceted soul with a deep commitment to knowledge, leadership, and innovation. Beyond his professional accomplishments, he finds inspiration in literature, the arts, and fitness, continually enriching his understanding of the world. His dedication to mental health, holistic healing, alternative medicine, and nutrition demonstrates his unwavering belief in the power of a balanced and health-focused lifestyle.

Through his work Dr. Frick provides a beacon of inspiration and guidance for those seeking financial abundance, holistic well-being, and a deeper connection to their authentic selves. His leadership exemplifies the transformative power of service, offering tools and motivation to those ready to embark on a journey of growth and self-discovery.

Whether you aspire to professional success, improved health, or a more meaningful life, Dr. Frick stands as a trusted guide and mentor. His life's mission is to inspire others, helping them unlock their full potential and embrace a future filled with purpose and fulfillment.

Connect with Dr. Frick at drstaceykevinfrick.com.

CHAPTER 17

PERSEVERANCE AND FAITH

The Road Map to Success

By Josephine Ozougwu

The mood of the room was tense.

The air, thick with judgment and disdain, marked a moment that would symbolize a divide in my family I never saw coming.

My mother's face, once so soft and full of love, was drawn tight with fury. My brother's voice, once a source of comfort, now rang with shocking threats that sliced through me like a knife. "If you don't stop this madness with Scripture Union, you're on your own. No school fees. No support," he spat, his eyes blazing with anger.

My mother, desperate and trembling, then spoke words that almost stopped my heart.

"If you don't renounce this faith of yours—I will kill myself," she cried.

It felt as though the ground beneath me had crumbled. This was my family, the people who had once showered me with love and protection. Now it seemed that their faces contorted with betrayal. I was twelve years old when I chose to follow Christ and join Scripture Union, and over the years, my faith had deepened, forging a conviction that even the threat of isolation could not cut through. Still, the thought of losing them broke my heart. Our home had been filled with love, music, and laughter, and now it would all be ripped away from me simply because I had followed my heart. "I will not turn back," I whispered to myself. Tears welled in my eyes, but they were not tears of defeat. They were born of a faith that had taken root deep in my soul and refused to be uprooted, no matter how fierce the judgment against it. The days that followed were a blur.

My brother's threats hung over me like a shadow, and my mother's desperate pleas haunted my nights. But I clung to God's promises like a lifeline. When I took my college entrance exams, I poured my faith into every answer. Gaining admission to the University of Ife felt like a beacon of hope, but that light was quickly dimmed when my English results were withheld. And when they were finally released, the news was crushing: I had not passed. I left the university in defeat, my dreams momentarily shattered, but when I retook the exams in Lagos, Nigeria, by the grace of God I passed! With my admission to the University of Nigeria, Nsukka, a new chapter began—one written by God's hand. The question of who would sponsor my education lingered, a daunting uncertainty that threatened to undo my resolve. Yet once again, providence intervened. An unexpected scholarship covered my studies in education biology. It was a sign that I was not walking this path alone. It was also in Lagos that I met the man who would become my husband.

On July 31, 1983, we were married in Enugu, a union that brought love and stability to my life. Within three years we were blessed with three children: our firstborn, Ngozi Gift, and twins, Chukwuebuka and Chinenye. Life's blessings were beginning to outweigh its trials. Little did I know that the most profound trials and redemptions were yet to come.

Fighting Giants: Hopelessness to Hopefulness

Two armies faced each other across the field, their faces hard and determined. David, a young shepherd with no fighting experience, had been chosen to lead this charge against the fierce and giant Goliath.

No one was betting on David, but he remembered his past

victories over a raging lion, and that memory, coupled with his faith in God, led him to victory. More than once I have felt like David, small and inexperienced but strong in my determination to keep going. After all, I had learned that even if my mother and father were willing to forsake me, the Lord would always pick me up and give me the grace to handle the giants that came my way. And come they surely did!

In 1987 we left Nigeria for the US, initially settling in Virginia before relocating to Houston. Adapting to our new home presented challenges, including finding jobs and housing. My first job was as an armed security guard, a role for which I had neither prior training nor skills. Understanding my instructor was difficult due to his accent, and I had to focus intently to comprehend the material. My lack of experience was evident during the practical competency test at the shooting range, where I fell backward upon pulling the trigger. "Sorry," the supervisor said, "this isn't going to work." I couldn't bear the thought of being the reason my family would struggle, but thankfully my husband, recognizing our desperate situation, pleaded with my supervisor to grant me a second chance. God answered our prayers, and I passed the test on my second attempt, securing the job.

Managing the arrival of our fourth child, Cheta, and balancing a forty-hour workweek as a security guard with nursing school was hectic, as I commuted an hour each way, but we persevered. Things began to ease off. After becoming a licensed registered nurse, I left my security job for a night-shift position at a hospital, which allowed me to be available for our children during the day. My husband found a job as a chemical analyst, and within a few years we started our home-health agency and bakery businesses. The grace of God and the unwavering support of my husband were crucial to our success. After an eight-year hiatus from having babies, God blessed us with a surprise fifth child, Joseph. His arrival brought unexpected stress but immense joy.

Lesson: Our ways are not God's ways. However, His ways are the best.

Anytime you find yourself on an unexpected road, can you allow yourself to believe that you have been put there for a divine reason? Can you trust that a higher plan is always at work, holding your hand and helping you live your most purposeful life?

As I look back on my journey, I see the fingerprints of God in every victory and every challenge. Like David, I faced my giants not with the confidence of experience but with the certainty of faith. I would need that faith for what was about to happen.

TRUSTING THE WILL OF GOD

"Don't touch me!" my husband screamed as I knelt beside him.

A moment before, I had heard my daughter's voice calling my name in a panic. "Mom, come quick; dad is calling for you from the bathroom." When I got there, I found my husband on the floor in excruciating pain. My hands were shaking as I tried to dial the phone, my brain struggling to remember how to call 911.

What followed was a whirlwind of chaos, the ambulance rushing him to the hospital for a barrage of tests that brought devastating news.

"Your husband has stage IV cancer, multiple myeloma," the doctor said sympathetically. "He has one month to live."

Suddenly everything was a blur. He kept talking, but his words sounded muffled to me as my head spun in denial. "Don't tell me that," I pleaded. "We have children and businesses. We have a life. A good life." My husband was my hero, my encourager, and the driving force behind our businesses. He was the primary breadwinner, an amazing father, and a wonderful husband who helped me with the children. The thought of losing him was unbearable.

Our life seemed to flash before me. Memories of the past and dreams of the future rushed through my mind, and somewhere in that scene a thought took root. I would find a way to work from home. I would help my husband heal. We were not going to accept this death sentence. We trusted that the will of God was far more powerful than the will of man. And we were right.

FAITH DELIVERS

As we prayed and trusted God for direction, doors began to open. My husband was admitted to MD Anderson Hospital, the number one cancer center in the nation, where he received treatment including chemotherapy, radiation, surgery, medication, and physical and occupational therapy. The staff and doctors were incredible. We coveted the prayers of our churches, fellowships, friends, and children, which were priceless. Studying the Word of God, eating organic foods, exercising, avoiding stress, and creating a peaceful environment became second nature to us.

Managing our businesses was a concern, but God provided a solution through a home-based business called Ambit Energy, an electricity company. My nursing career, while rewarding, had been stressful, especially with four of our children in college simultaneously and my husband requiring total care. Ambit allowed me to work from home and alleviate some of the pressure. When I first introduced the opportunity to my husband, he was skeptical, but as he saw the results, he became my biggest supporter. Through my success with Ambit we were able to provide for my husband's care and build a legacy for our family. In fact, I reached the position of executive consultant and became one of Ambit's millionaire club members. Twice while I was working from home, my husband's heart stopped and God, through my CPR training, brought him back to life. It hit me then how the dots of my life were divinely connected.

I hadn't imagined I would become a nurse, but then God used my training and saved my husband. I hadn't imagined I would work for an energy company, but doing so supported my family. Every step I had taken had equipped me to be exactly who I needed to be at each phase of life! Imagine knowing that not a single thing you have done has been a waste. Imagine trusting that every detour you've taken was actually deliberate guidance from God, moving you into the exact place you needed to be to live your destiny!

It was eighteen years ago we received that diagnosis. My husband is still alive today. Man said he had one month to live. God gave us eighteen years and counting. I hope you remember that the next time man says no, God can say yes. When man says, "Impossible," God sends miracles. Ultimately, where the devil constructs roadblocks, God can clear the way for you. But you must be confident, never abandoning one another in the face of the fiercest battles, because any soldier that endures to the end receives a medal of honor.

THE MELODY OF LIFE

Life is like a symphony, its tones rising and falling, the melody light and joyful one moment, and dark and brooding the next. One shift in key, and everything changes—just like life. It's a masterpiece of contrasts, where harmony is found in trusting the composer—God! Throughout my life I have adopted three mantras, and I live by them every day:

1. I will never let anyone or anything steal my joy.

2. I will always exalt God above my problems.

3. I will always leave someone or something better than when I met them.

No matter how daunting the adversity is, triumph is always within reach. You become truly unstoppable when you trust God, give your best, surround yourself with positive people, practice gratitude, prioritize self-care, celebrate your wins, and never quit. As the scripture says, "Now thanks be unto God, which always causeth us to triumph in Christ" (2 Cor. 2:14, kjv). With God and the right people by your side there is no challenge too great for you to overcome. My life has been a testimony to the miracle of faith. We endured so many challenges but have also been given so many blessings.

Our five fabulous children have all graduated from college,

with some earning master's and doctorate degrees. Four are married with children. Our two sons even played in the NFL. We are blessed with thirteen wonderful grandchildren, and more are on the way. My brave husband, once declared incurable and given just a month to live, has been granted eighteen years and counting by God's grace. This year marks forty-two years of a happy and loving marriage. And my mother, the woman who had once threatened to end her life over my faith, began to change. Slowly she opened her heart to Christ. Before her passing she embraced the very faith she had so vehemently opposed, her transformation a testament to the power of time and grace. My story is a song of resilience that began in the midst of familial betrayal and grew into a symphony of redemption and love. It is proof that even in the darkest moments God's light shines through, guiding us to a future we never could have imagined.

Life, like music, is a dynamic, ever-changing composition. Each note, each rest, and every crescendo contribute to its beauty. Trust the composer of your life's symphony. The melody of victory is already yours—now go and play it boldly and with faith!

About Josephine

Energy Specialist | Advocate for Financial Freedom | Transformational Trainer

Josephine Ozougwu is an energy specialist dedicated to empowering individuals and businesses to save on electricity, gas, and solar solutions. With extensive knowledge and experience, she focuses on innovative strategies that help clients access free electricity and create income opportunities, guiding them toward financial stability and sustainability.

Originally from Enugu, Nigeria, Josephine's educational journey began at Queens School Enugu, followed by the University of Nigeria, Nsukka, where she earned a degree in education biology. Her passion for helping others led her to Pasadena Nursing School, where she trained as a nurse. This unique blend of education and experience allows her to approach her work with expertise and compassion.

Josephine owned a home-health agency, El Shaddai Care Services Inc., for over twenty years. She is also a certified Transformational Trainer through Lisa Nichols, equipping her with the skills to inspire and motivate others. As a devoted mother of five and grandmother of thirteen, she has been a caregiver for over eighteen years, embodying the values of commitment, love, and joy, which she strives to pass on to her family.

Now residing in Houston, Josephine enjoys dancing, personal development, singing, gardening, and traveling. She believes in cherishing every moment of life and the importance of enjoying the journey. Her mission is to glorify God daily by helping others fulfill their dreams and achieve generational wealth.

Josephine expresses deep gratitude for the support of her family, mentors, and friends who have significantly impacted her journey. She acknowledges her brother and mentor, Bro Godfrey Ukoh, for his invaluable wisdom, as well as Bishop Arthur and Dr. Gina Ojionuka for their hospitality during her transition to the US.

This chapter is dedicated to her wonderful family, who stood by her through thick and thin. Josephine aims to transform challenges into triumphs, inspiring others to embrace their potential and create a brighter future for themselves and their families. Join her on this journey of empowerment and transformation!

Learn more at JosephineOzougwu.com.

www.ingramcontent.com/pod-product-compliance
Lightning Source LLC
Chambersburg PA
CBHW070702190326
41458CB00046B/6814/J